M

Hasidic Tales

Other books in the
SkyLight Illuminations Series

Hasidic Tales

Annotated & Explained

Translation & Annotation
by Rabbi Rami Shapiro

Foreword by Andrew Harvey

Walking Together, Finding the Way
SKYLIGHT PATHS Publishing
Woodstock, Vermont

Hasidic Tales:
Annotated & Explained

First Printing 2004
Translation, annotation, and introductory material © 2004 by Rami Shapiro
Foreword © 2004 by Andrew Harvey

For information regarding permission to reprint material from this book, please mail or fax your request in writing to SkyLight Paths Publishing, Permissions Department, at the address/fax number listed below, or e-mail your request to permissions@skylightpaths.com.

Library of Congress Cataloging-in-Publication Data

Shapiro, Rami M.
Hasidic tales : annotated & explained / translation and annotation by Rami Shapiro.
     p. cm. — (SkyLight illuminations)
Includes bibliographical references.
ISBN 1-893361-86-1 (pbk.)
1. Hasidim—Legends. 2. Rabbis—Legends. 3. Legends, Jewish.
4. Hasidism. I. Title. II. Series.
BM532 .S485 2003
296.8'332—dc22

                                                  2003015351

10 9 8 7 6 5 4 3 2 1

Manufactured in the United States of America

SkyLight Paths Publishing is creating a place where people of different spiritual traditions come together for challenge and inspiration, a place where we can help each other understand the mystery that lies at the heart of our existence.

SkyLight Paths sees both believers and seekers as a community that increasingly transcends traditional boundaries of religion and denomination—people wanting to learn from each other, *walking together, finding the way.*

Walking Together, Finding the Way
Published by SkyLight Paths Publishing
A Division of LongHill Partners, Inc.
Sunset Farm Offices, Route 4, P.O. Box 237
Woodstock, VT 05091
Tel: (802) 457-4000   Fax: (802) 457-4004
www.skylightpaths.com

Contents □

Foreword ☐

Andrew Harvey

"It is joy that reveals our true nature."
—*The Rebbe of Hanipoli*

Many years ago when I was a fellow of All Souls College at Oxford, I was invited by the Israeli government, along with a group of other writers and intellectuals, to visit Israel. It was one of the happiest journeys I ever undertook, mostly because, towards the end, I met a Hasid whom I will call "Isaiah." This wild middle-aged Russian Jew, whose hilarity, passion, wit, and sense of the holy in all things—from the way sunlight hit the stones of old walls to the sweetness of stray cats—astonished me and lifted me up from the young man's despair and cynicism I was mired in.

I met Isaiah at a rambunctious conference of poets, artists, and seekers in old Jerusalem. We immediately became friends. I loved his exuberant Einstein-haired appearance; his flights of quote-studded mystical passion; the surreal way he dressed in old sneakers, tattered purple and pink tee shirt, and baggy black pants out of a pirate film. He appointed himself quickly as my guide to the "real" Jerusalem and to the "real" Jewish mysticism, and I spent two timeless days rambling and laughing with him around the old city. I listened to his stories and imbibed from the way he talked and occasionally burst into song or prayer some of the vibrant spontaneity of the tradition he loved with all his heart. Many years later when I read the famous Hasidic story about how the Rabbi Leib went to study with the Mezritcher Rebbe not to learn Torah but "to watch him tie and untie his shoelaces," I immediately thought of Isaiah and smiled. He had a way of patting my shoulder or ruffling my hair, pulling out a chair for me to sit on or stirring lumps of sugar into my thick local coffee, that was breathtaking in its intimate sweetness and in the sense it gave me of his warm and tender respect, not just for me but for all beings. One of my happiest memories of Isaiah is of watching him, near the Wailing Wall, bow to a mangy old dog whose left ear had almost been bitten off in a recent fight. "Old warrior," he said as he bowed, "I salute you! May God bless you." The dog that had been snarling and cowering suddenly fell quiet and gazed up at him with something like wonder.

Isaiah radiated so much natural joy I was astonished when he told me at the end of our first evening together that he had been in Auschwitz as a child. It seemed impossible to me that someone who had seen and known such final desolation could now be living in such obvious—and contagious—love for life. I told him so and he smiled. "God is in hell, too," he said gently. "Some of my fellow Hasidim in the camp went to their deaths in the gas chamber singing and dancing."

I did not tell him at the time but what he said about his fellow Hasidim "singing and dancing" their way to certain death disturbed and even repulsed me. How could "singing and dancing" be a response to such horror and butchery? Were the Hasidim crazy? Was the tradition that had shaped such a response—one that claimed to be inspired by God— in fact rooted in denial and an almost obscene ignorance of the truth and power of evil? I was a young man much preoccupied by the brutality of the civilization I had been born into, profoundly pessimistic about human nature, and so appalled by what I had learned about the Holocaust that I could hardly bear to read books about it for fear of losing what little remained in me of hope and trust in life. For a long sleepless night, I wrestled with what Isaiah had told me. As dawn broke, I decided I would have to ask him to explain himself. I did not want to challenge him. Rather, I wanted with my whole being to know why, in his opinion, the Hasidim had danced, and what that meant for him. The next day we met for lunch in a quiet sun-drenched square not far from the Via Golgotha. As soon as we sat down, I leaned forward, fixed Isaiah with my best British stare, and said coldly, "Last night, you told me of the Hasidim you knew who had gone to the gas chambers dancing."

"Yes," he said, looking at his hands.

"Well, how do you know they weren't deluded? *If* they weren't deluded, what on earth could such a gesture have meant? Did they accept the horror of what was being done to them? And if so, doesn't such an acceptance condone evil and ensure its victory?"

Isaiah first whistled softly then fell silent, closing his eyes. He began, "You know, of course, that Hasidism is a Jewish religious movement that began in the eighteenth century and swept through parts of Poland and Russia and engendered a whole galaxy of teachers and mystics, even more fervent and impassioned and numerous than the one in Safed two centuries earlier. And you know, I imagine, that the word *Hasidism* is derived from the word *hesed.*"

"Yes," I nodded, "and *hesed* means compassion."

"No!" Isaiah cried out. "Compassion is too cold a translation! Compassion is too English a word for the passionate, ecstatic, tender loving-kindness that the Jewish mystics mean when they say *hesed.* Think of a forge. Let that stand for your spiritual practice. And now imagine a worker and his tools. And let that stand for you and your devoted intentions—your *kavvanah*—to practice with all your heart so as to reach and experience God. What is lacking? A spark to ignite and get the whole forge blazing, Andrew. Something more than compassion is needed; something so passionate and fiery, something that is nothing less than that part of the blissful fire of God's love for all things that is your heart-core. That passionate bliss-fire is *hesed.*"

Isaiah went on to explain that *hesed,* this bliss-fire of Divine Love, underpins the whole of the universe and is boundless like the heart it streams from forever. Every bird, every stone, every fern, every dancing flea is burning in its flame—it is the flame-stuff from which all the universe is woven in ecstasy. In Hebrew, the root word for love is *A-H-V*. Usually, it is pronounced *ahavah* but Hebrew grammar, which has no vowels, allows us to break it down into two words, *eh-hav*. And *eh-hav* means "I will give." God gives the burning love of *hesed* to us constantly at all times, and in all circumstances. That is what you come to know when your heart is opened in awe and humility to the Creator. Infinite love is given; it is the nature of God to give it infinitely. A Hasid knows this and dares to try to empty himself or herself so as to be filled with the divine passion of compassion and blaze with its rapture and hunger to serve all beings in the Real.

One of Isaiah's favorite Hasidic masters, Rebbe Schlomo Carlebach, was famous for shouting at his Hasidim: "Don't you know you have to be drunk on God? So get drunk, now! Where is the drunkenness I am talking of? It is a wine burning in your heart! I need Hasidim who are drunk on love!" True Hasidim are those who have allowed themselves to experience the drunkenness of God's love for us, for Creation, and for all things of Creation. Rebbe Schneur Zalman, the founder of a school of Hasidic thought that later came to be known as the Lubavitcher Movement, said, "Even in the inorganic things such as stones or dust or water there is to be found the quality of soul and spiritual life." True Hasidim are those who become drunk themselves—drunk with awe, humility, reverence for the Presence of God in everything; drunk on the goodness and mercy of God that, however terrible things seem, are always working for the perfection of the world. To be drunk in this way requires profound sacred passion and a whole way of life that tries to live each moment as sacred. The Baal Shem Tov, the founder of Hasidism and perhaps its greatest teacher, said, quoting from the Psalms, "In all of your ways, know God." To a Hasid, this means that in all you do—eating, walking, talking, making love—you should strive with your whole being to consecrate your actions and so savor God's bliss in them.

To live like this requires far more than emotion. It requires the most intense imaginable discipline of the heart, a constant turning of the heart toward celebration, praise, a direct seeing and knowing of *Ayn Sof*—the Infinite One—in all things and events. It is far more difficult to live a life of true joy than it is to live one of misery and depression. True joy requires a constant emptying of yourself before God, a continual commitment to go beyond whatever you imagine to be the facts of even the most terrible situation to celebrate the power and source from which it comes and the mystery of mercy hidden within it. True joy requires the most ruthless and realistic humility, because only the truly humble can be empty enough to be filled constantly by the bliss-fire of the *hesed* of God.

Isaiah illustrated the depth of this discipline, this abundance of joy, by telling one of his favorite stories. There was a very holy man, a master of *hesed,* called the Ropchitzer Rebbe. One evening, he and his disciples were dancing. Suddenly, the old Rebbe raised his arms with an expression of great pain on his face. His disciples noticed that he was suffering and stopped dancing. This made the old Rebbe furious and he cried out, stamping his feet, "Does an army stop the struggle when a general dies? Keep dancing, keep dancing!" It was only a few days later that the disciples learned that an old friend of the Rebbe's, the Kamarner Rebbe, had died at the very moment the Ropchitzer Rebbe had raised his arms.

It may seem strange that the Ropchitzer Rebbe referred to his disciples as "an army" and the ecstatic devotion they were plunged in as a "struggle." In fact, Isaiah explained, the Rebbe was revealing to his Hasidim the core secret of the Hasidic way. He was revealing to them that to live the truth of reality requires the most determined imaginable commitment to a struggle against anything—pride, grief, anger, depression, inner doubt, laziness of being—that keeps you from knowing and burning in God's joy. To become a Hasid is to become a blessing for others. You have to give yourself again and again and again to the great dance of praise and celebration, whatever the circumstances boiling around you. The Rebbe was telling his disciples—and himself, as, for a moment, the grief of losing his beloved friend shadowed him—to "keep dancing!" To keep dancing in the way the Rebbe meant is not a denial of death, pain, horror, or evil. It is a continual and ultimate affirmation of the mercy, power, and *hesed* of God, of the essential truth of life. To keep dancing is a continual reimmersion in the fire of God's glory to be turned slowly to pure gold in its frames.

Isaiah's Rebbe, who loved the Ropchitzer Rebbe and this story, used to say again and again, "The universe is dancing and we are here to dance that dance with it and for the Creator." For him, as for all true Hasidim, the whole aim of every practice and *mitzvos* (commandments) is to experience *d'veikus,* which means the most passionate love when you are not separated from the Infinite for even a moment. Not to be separated from the Infinite for even a moment is to be always inwardly dancing in the bliss of the Infinite, whatever orgy of evil or cruelty is reveling in the outer world, even if you are shattered, heartbroken, and dying. In Proverbs 16:6, it is said, "The one who pursues loving-kindness…finds life." The deepest meaning of this is that the one who keeps *hesed* alive within himself or herself through everything comes to live the divine life on earth. The one who keeps *hesed* aflame comes to share the forgiveness and tenderness of the life of God, even in hell.

Isaiah paused and took my hand in his. "And now, Andrew, you understand why some of the Hasidim were singing and dancing on the way to the ovens."

I could say nothing. All my cleverness seemed frivolous and absurd before the truths he had shared with me.

Isaiah released my hand, leaned back in his chair, and smiled. "I often think that another reason why some of the Hasidim in the camp were dancing to their deaths was that they knew that even if they were going to die, the truth of the Hasidic tradition could not be killed. It is the truth of the path of divine love itself and transcends all religion. It is always there to be discovered and lived by those crazy and devoted enough!"

Today, there is a revival of Hasidism and Kabbalah starting in America and in the West. The dance goes on! The West is in the grip of Kabbalahfever. A torrent of books—some excellent, some exploitative—is making the ancient esoteric wisdom of Judaism available to any serious seeker. This is great and glorious good news. Kabbalistic mysticism has radiant treasures of vision and knowledge to share with anyone willing to study and open to them. The danger inherent in this release of esoteric information, however, is if the approach to it is limited to the intellectual. Kabbalah, in its intricacy and complexity, can encourage the kind of semi-elitist mental excitation that blocks rather than furthers the authentic mystical journey which is always a journey into ever-greater nakedness of being and humility.

This is where the Hasidic tradition can be of help. In it, as the stories of this wonderful book make clear, divine knowledge is always rooted in the details of ordinary life. The aim of all knowledge or visionary ecstasy is to increase the power of *hesed* and compassionate action. The wisdom of the Hasidim is earthy, realistic, rooted in the simplicity of the heart. It is alive with the awareness of the holiness of Creation and the boundlessness of God's mercy, and is utterly honest about the necessity of living such awareness in loving service to all beings. It is a wisdom that fuses the highest mystical initiations with the most down-home celebration of life and a rugged commitment to social and political justice in all its forms. In other words, it is a wisdom that is never, as my old school headmaster would put it, "too divine to be of any earthly use."

There is nothing sentimental about these ancient stories or about the vision that inspired them. The Hasidic masters were fiercely alert to the subtlety of evil and the power of pride and conceit to taint even our highest longings and corrupt even our highest ideals. Their relentless emphasis on the true divine life showed them to be free of that grandiose rhetoric that so often distorts the well-meaning intentions of the New Age. Their quest for union with God was far too serious for them to think of glamorizing it. They knew that with great knowledge and love came great responsibility to try to represent the Divine in all things and activities, and to stand up for justice and the dispossessed in a brutal society. They knew that God gave the human race divine identity. They knew too the possibilities this opened up for the co-creation with God of an ever more perfect world, and were brave enough to embrace the price of authentic transformation.

It is this realism of the Hasidic masters—both in the sense of being mystically open to the bliss and splendor of the Real and of being unsentimentally aware of the deviousness of the human psyche, the harshness of the world, and the rigor of divine service—that makes them such reliable guides and makes their stories as relevant today as when they were first told. We believe the Hasidic Rebbes and their disciples because we hear in what they say and read in what they do the signs of wisdom honed by humility. We believe in their exaltation because it is won from pain, doubt, and unwavering knowledge of injustice. We celebrate their ecstasy because we see it drove them not to a selfish seclusion from the world but to an extravagant and courageous witness within it of the fullness of joy that Psalm 16 affirms is the truth of the "path of life" when lived "in thy presence."

In a dangerous and heartbroken time like ours, when the entire survival of the human race and of nature is at stake, and when every week the media affords us new reasons to tremble and despair, the unwavering emphasis in these stories on the divine glory given to human beings who are willing to give themselves entirely to God reminds us of who we are and of who we can still be, if we are brave, wild, tender, and "drunken" enough. Nothing is more important in a time like this than to "keep dancing," to keep giving away everything of ourselves to other beings in a spirit of *hesed* and in that ecstasy of selfless service that the Hasidic Rebbes and their disciples knew and incarnated with such humor and fervent abandon.

Let these wonderful old masters of the Dance inspire you now!

Preface □

I have been in love with stories and storytelling since I was a little boy hiding under the bedcovers at night to read long after my parents had ordered me to go to sleep. I started writing stories when I was eleven, my first being a retelling of Noah and the Flood, my second a sci-fi take on the splitting of the Red Sea. In high school my friend Bob Bessel and I created a literary journal called *The Rat* to use poetry and fiction to correct the injustices of the world—or at least the horrid conditions in the school cafeteria. It was clear to me that stories could change things. It took several more years before I realized they could transform people.

In 1970 I was a sophomore at Tel Aviv University, editor of the school's English-language newspaper, and a student of Hasidism and Kabbalah. I enjoyed my academic study of Jewish mysticism, but I wanted more. I wanted "to taste and see" for myself that God was good (Psalm 34:8). I began to spend time with the HaBaD Hasidim that came to campus every Friday to get male students to put on *tefillin* (phylacteries).

These young men, with their long *payis* (sidecurls), black suits with white tieless shirts buttoned at the neck, and black hats at least two sizes too small for their pale and close-cropped heads, were all too eager to make me a convert. They found me to be a sponge for their stories and their teachings. I lived briefly at Kvar HaBaD, their Hasidic village, where I studied the *Tanya*, the foundational text of HaBaD written by the Alter Rebbe, Rabbi Schneur Zalman of Liadi. I could not get enough of their wisdom, but soon I had had enough of them. I loved their teaching but could not fit myself into their lifestyle.

While at Kvar HaBaD I heard about Reb Reuven, a renegade rabbi without standing in any official community, who had gotten permission from the

Israeli government to create a kibbutz for non-Orthodox Jews looking to study Kabbalah. I recruited a couple of friends from the university, and the three of us went off to volunteer at this new kabbalistic kibbutz.

Reb Reuven was a messianic character with the kind of charismatic personality that could do either great good or great evil. I have written about some of my experiences with him in a series of short stories called *Messiah Man*, published in Penninah Schram's book *Chosen Tales*. My friends and I became poster boys for his kibbutz, appearing in an Israeli newsreel shown in movie theaters throughout the country. We would join his community on Fridays, spend *Shabbos* (Sabbath) in prayer, meditation, and study, and then help clear the land on Sundays. One *Shabbos* afternoon he called me into his study. He was sitting behind his desk and motioned me to take the chair across from him. A volume of the *Zohar* was lying open in front of him.

"Do you know what the *Zohar* is?" he asked.

"Of course," I said. "It is a mystical commentary on Torah written by Moshe deLeon, a thirteenth-century Spanish kabbalist who...."

"Nonsense!" he screamed at me, half rising out of his chair. "The *Zohar* isn't just a commentary; it's a Torah all by itself. It is a new Torah, a new telling of the last Torah. You do know what Torah is, don't you?"

Suspecting that I didn't, and afraid to invoke his wrath a second time, I waited silently, certain that he would answer his own question. I was not disappointed.

"Torah is story. God is story. Israel is story. You, my dear university-educated soon-to-be a liberal pain in the ass rabbi, are a story. We are all stories! We are all Torahs!"

He paused, expecting me to respond, but I was unclear as to which part of his statement I was to respond to. I had no plans to be a rabbi. I was in Israel to placate a haunting sense of guilt about being so involved in Buddhist studies. It would be years before my Zen master, Joshu Sasaki Roshi, would push me toward the rabbinate. But that is another story.

"Listen, Rami," Reuven said in a softer voice. "Torah starts with the

word *bereshit,* 'Once upon a time!' Torah is God's storybook; God is a storyteller! Torah tells us that God created the world through speech. What
kind of speech? Stories. He told the story of light, and there was light.
He told the story of heaven and earth, and they came into being. Torah
says God breathed into Adam, the first human. What did God breathe?
Stories! Stories bring things alive, not once and forever but every time
they are told.

"Stories transcend time and space. Stories reveal the deepest truths of
life, the greatest sorrows, the highest joys. And they do so not by telling
you anything but by showing you everything. God could have given
Moses a law book on Mount Sinai. Instead, He gave a storybook and
stuck the laws in among them! Nobody is going to read the law over and
over again unless they are trying to find a way out of abiding by it. But
stories—stories we cannot stop telling. And when we do, they are no
longer stories about the ancients but stories about ourselves.

"That is why the ancient Rabbis told stories. That is why Jesus told
stories. That is why Shakespeare told stories. That is why the Bhagavad
Gita is a story. That is why the *Zohar* is a story. That is why Reb Nachman told stories. That is why we Hasidim tell stories. That is why..."

Reb Reuven stopped speaking for a moment and gave me a wry smile.
"What, you think I don't know from Jesus and Krishna and Shakespeare?
You think I am afraid of them? A good storyteller isn't afraid of any story.
On the contrary, a good storyteller—a teller who tells tales to awaken
the soul—seeks out the good stories wherever they are found and honors
the tellers whoever they are. You will see. One day you will be a storyteller. You will tell the tales of Jesus and Krishna, Buddha and Chuang
Tzu—yes, you see I know these things—and you will tell the stories of
your own people as well: the Besht [Baal Shem Tov], the *Maggid*
[Preacher] of Mezritch, Reb Nachman, the *tzaddikim* [Hasidic masters],
even that *apikorus* [heretic] Martin Buber. This is why you are here. Do
you think I need another hand to till the soil? So, good, you work the land,
but you are here to learn the stories."

Reb Reuven suddenly grew very tired. He sank into his chair, his shoulders falling forward and his chest caving a bit toward his stomach. He pulled the *Zohar* closer to him and smiled at me. He waved his hand as if swatting a fly and said, "Go, go. Enough ranting for one *Shabbos*. But don't forget what I have told you. The secret to everything is in its story."

I did not forget. Nor have I ever doubted the truth of what he taught me. The secret to everything is in its story. As a rabbi, counselor, and spiritual guide, I know that story is key. The stories we tell ourselves about ourselves determine the quality of the selves we imagine we are. The stories we tell about others determine the quality of our relationships with them. Stories are more than memory. Stories are creative acts of world-making. When we tell a story about ourselves we create the self about which we are talking. The veracity of the story has nothing to do with its historicity and everything to do with the accuracy with which it reveals the subtle psychospiritual dynamic at work in the storyteller and the story listener.

The tales in this collection are true in this way. They speak to the heart and of the soul. They are deep teaching tales told by the Hasidim about those masters of the spirit who lived life in the Presence of God. I offer them here in honor of those who revealed them to me. It is my way of thanking them by passing on the gift they gave me. I hope you will read them not as stories about Hasidism but as stories of Hasidim about life.

Ever since meeting Stuart M. Matlins, I have wanted to work with him, and Jewish Lights, the sister company of SkyLight Paths, the publisher of this book. The fact that he came to me with the suggestion for this book means more to me than he will ever know. The fact that the series in which this book appears is edited by my friend and teacher, Andrew Harvey, a man who is the living embodiment of what it means to be a God-intoxicated Hasid despite the fact that there is absolutely nothing Jewish about him, made this project all the more sweet. I am deeply grateful to these two men for all they have given me. I am grateful as well to Jon Sweeney of SkyLight Paths, whose efforts to sharpen the focus and presentation of these tales was an invaluable aid, and to my editor Emily Wichland, whose tireless efforts to make this book the best it could be transformed my rough-cut stones into what I hope you will find to be gleaming gems. To you all, my heartfelt thanks.

This book is dedicated to Reb Zalman Schachter–Shalomi, my rebbe, my way-pointer, and my friend.

Introduction ☐

When faced with a particularly weighty problem, the Baal Shem Tov, founder of Hasidic Judaism, would go to a certain place in the woods, light a sacred fire, and pray. In this way, he found insight into his dilemma. His successor, Rabbi Dov Ber, the Preacher of Mezritch, followed his example and went to the same place in the woods and said, "The fire we can no longer light, but we can still say the prayer." And he, too, found what he needed. Another generation passed, and Rabbi Moshe Leib of Sassov went to the woods and said, "The fire we can no longer light, the prayer we no longer remember; all we know is the place in the woods, and that will have to suffice." And it did. In the fourth generation, Rabbi Israel of Rishin stayed at home and said, "The fire we can no longer light, the prayer we no longer know, nor do we remember the place. All we can do is tell the tale." And that, too, proved sufficient.

But why? Why is it that telling the story carries the same healing power as the original act? Because the story recreates the act in such a way as to invite us into it. We don't simply listen to a story; we become the story. The very act of giving our attention to the story gives the story a personal immediacy that erases the boundary between the story and ourselves.

Although the power of the story to engage the listener is not unique to Jews, it is explicit in Judaism. Each spring at the Passover seder, a storied re-creation of the Exodus from Egypt, participants are urged to tell the tale as if they themselves were experiencing the events right there in their own homes. The Passover story is not a recounting of what happened once upon a time; it is a "live broadcast" spoken by observers "embedded" in the events themselves.

Storytelling, far more than sacrifice and law, is at the heart of Judaism. Rashi (an acronym for Rabbi Shlomo Yitzchak), the famous eleventh-century Jewish sage, asks in his commentary on the Torah why Torah doesn't begin with the revelation at Sinai but instead begins with and includes the tales of creation, Cain and Abel, the Tower of Babel, and the legends of Abraham. Rashi answers that this is done to make it clear that God is the God of all creation and can do with it as God sees fit. But there is a less theological reason that I find far more convincing. If the Bible focused on law and commandments rather than embedding them in drama and storytelling, it would be much more difficult to get people to read it. It is the story that carries the law, not the law that carries the story.

Humans are storytelling animals. From the moment we awake to the moment we go to sleep, our primary means of communication is the story. Our stories define us, instruct us, create us. Without our stories, we do not exist, as the sad plight of amnesia sufferers makes so very clear. For us, our story is our self.

When you see friends on Monday morning and someone asks you what you did over the weekend, you don't pull out your Palm Pilot or Pocket PC and read the appointments listed in your calendar. You tell a story: "Sunday morning started out normal enough, but on my way to the grocery store there was this incredible car accident, and I rushed over to help. You won't believe who was in the car...." The same is true when you meet with family or friends at the end of a day and relate what happened at home, work, or school. Unless you are a teenager talking to an adult, the answer to "What did you do today?" is rarely "Nothing." You tell a story. And the story you tell determines the meaning you derive from the events of your life.

The quality of our lives depends to a great degree on the kinds of stories we tell. Miserable people tend to tell stories of woe; joyous people tend to tell stories of hope. The question we must ask is this: Do our tales reflect the personality of the teller, or do they create it? Does the tale mirror the teller, or does the teller come to resemble the tale?

The safest answer, of course, is that it is a bit of both. But my own experience as a congregational rabbi and professional storyteller is that the tale has greater power than the teller. This is why so many of the great spiritual teachers told stories. These are the great parables, the Zen *koan*, and the teaching tales of the world's wisdom traditions. Listening to these tales with full attention lifts us out of our own story and reveals an alternative drama that may offer us a greater sense of meaning than any of the tales we tell ourselves.

These tales shift our attention from the mundane to the holy while leaving us firmly grounded in the ordinary realities of our everyday lives. The most powerful teaching tales never take us out of the world but plant us more deeply in it. While often dealing with matters of the spirit, they continually ground us in the facts of daily living, for heaven and earth, nirvana and samsara, this world and the World to Come are simply different ways of experiencing the singular reality of this very moment. And that is what great stories do: They show us a different way to engage reality. Nothing changes but our minds, and this, of course, changes everything.

The stories I have collected were not chosen at random. They were not chosen to give you a sense of Hasidic life and teaching. They were not chosen to teach you about anything at all. They were chosen because when you listen to them carefully they will no longer be Hasidic stories; they will be your stories. They will no longer be about long-dead saints and sages; they will be about you. And when you hear what the story has to say about you, your life, and how best to live it, the story will have fulfilled its mission.

Although each of the stories in this small collection has been printed in various Hebrew collections of Hasidic tales and teachings, they were all originally oral tales. My versions of these tales are not literal translations from the Hebrew; to translate literally would have left you with sentences but no story. Stories such as these should not be translated but retold, and that is what I have attempted to do.

My goal is to tell these stories to you as they were told to me, and as I have told them over the past few decades. I have tried to retain both the easy flow of oral literature and the *yiddische tam,* the Eastern European flavor these stories carry. To manage the former, I often created dialogue where the sources offered only description. Dialogue slows the telling, heightens the drama, and allows us to learn the point along with the protagonists.

Regarding the latter, I chose to use the Ashkenazi (Eastern European) pronunciation of Hebrew rather than the now standard Sephardic (Spanish and Oriental) because these tales were originally told in Yiddish with Ashkenazi Hebrew insertions, and I wanted to pass on some of that flavor to you. The primary difference between the two is the use of a "t" sound in Sephardi Hebrew where the Ashkenazi prefers an "s." Thus, you will read about *Shabbos* rather than Shabbat, and *mitzvos* rather than mitzvot (commandments).

In addition to the annotations that go with each story, I have added my own commentary. This is drawn from my work as a spiritual guide. When people come to me to explore the intricacies of the spirit, I often share with them many of the stories in this book, adding comments similar to those that now accompany the stories as they appear here. I have chosen to include these commentaries to ensure that this book is not simply another collection of Hasidic tales but also a teaching text that you can use to further your own spiritual awakening. These are universal teaching tales told *through* a particular people of a particular faith at a particular time. Not only are these tales about wonder-working rabbis, their passionate disciples, and the laypeople who loved them, but they are also about your life and how you are to live it. Think of these stories not as texts to be studied but as the spiritual diary of an intimate friend who invites you to experience the world as she does by sharing with you the world she experiences.

I offer these tales to you as I have offered them to thousands of people throughout the past thirty years of my life as a storyteller and rabbi: as fingers pointing to the simple truth of living in the Presence of God. May you read and share these stories with an open heart so that they may do their work and reveal the glory of God and the challenge of godliness present here and now.

Hasidism, a Brief Introduction ☐

The ancient Rabbis taught, "God desires the heart." They themselves, however, seem to have preferred the head. Judaism has struggled through the ages to find a balance between heartfelt yearning for God and the intellectual mastery of God's Word. Generally speaking, it was the head that won out. Yet, when things got too heady, the pendulum would swing in favor of the heart. The eighteenth-century Jewish revivalist movement called Hasidism was one of these heart swings.

The founder of Hasidism was Israel ben Eliezer (1698–1760), who came to be called the Besht, an acronym for Baal Shem Tov, Master of the Good Name. *Baale Shem* (plural) were wonder workers, and the title "Baal Shem" tells us how they worked their wonders. "Baal" means "master," and "Shem," "name," refers to the Tetragrammaton, the four-letter Hebrew Name of God: *Yud, Hay, Vav, Hay,* or YHVH. Since early medieval times, Judaism celebrated Rabbis who had become masters of the Name—that is, scholar-mystics who could write the Name of God in amulets used to deepen one's spiritual life. Over time, and especially in Eastern Europe, the use of amulets became big business and attracted not only the saintly and pious but the charismatic con artist as well. *Baale Shem* wandered the countryside selling amulets to promote healing, conception, easy childbirth, and good fortune. To distinguish between quacks and authentic healers, people began to speak of Baal Shem Tov, Master of the Good Name, where the Hebrew *tov,* "good," let you know you were dealing with a healer of the highest integrity.

Orphaned as a child and raised as a ward of Okup, his native village in the Carpathian Mountains, Israel ben Eliezer was thought to be an ignoramus. In fact, he was a largely self-taught mystic skilled at keeping his learning a secret. Working as a school attendant, Israel would accompany the children to and from *cheder* (school), teaching them through melody and dance the joy of living in God's Presence.

The town eventually married him off to the sister of Rabbi Abraham Gershon of Kutow, who lived in the town of Brody. Reb Abraham was opposed to the marriage, having hoped his sister would find a scholar for a husband. After the wedding, Israel and his bride moved into Reb Abraham's house. It was then that the rabbi discovered the true nature of his new brother-in-law and became his disciple.

Before revealing himself as a teacher, Israel had been known as a healer, a Baal Shem. Given the efficacy of his amulets and quality of his person, he was known as the Baal Shem Tov, or the Besht, and this name stayed with him long after his healing work shifted from amulets to Hasidism.

A circle of disciples slowly formed around the Besht. Called the *chavurah kaddisha,* "holy company," this group of sages began to develop a highly sophisticated understanding of Judaism based not on the intellectual mastery of scholars but on the devout piety of the laity. The goal of the *chavurah kaddisha* was *d'veikus,* union with God.

The concept of *d'veikus* ("clinging" or "cleaving") is found in the Torah, where the verb *davak* signifies an extraordinary intimacy with the Divine: "To love YHVH your God, to listen to His voice and to cleave to Him, for He is your life and the length of your days..." (Deuteronomy 30:20). To achieve *d'veikus* is to realize that God is your life. While later Hasidic masters spoke of *d'veikus* as a union with God requiring the dissolution of the self, this was not the original understanding. God is your life, but your life is still yours; that is, Torah speaks of *d'veikus* as an experience of feeling the fullness of God present in your self without actually erasing your sense of self.

The Besht, in contrast to the Rabbis and their focus on scholarship and study, taught that *d'veikus* was the ultimate goal of the religious life. More radically, he taught that *d'veikus* was not reserved for the rare mystic who had mastered the esoteric lore and Torah commentaries of the

Kabbalah but was a state of mind that even the least educated could achieve, providing they would surrender themselves to the joy of serving God through the *mitzvos* (commandments) of Judaism.

The Baal Shem Tov did not reveal a systematic philosophy to his students. He taught instead by means of original aphorisms and proverbs. These his disciples wrote down, interpreted, and developed into a system of thought and practice that came to be called Hasidism, from the Hebrew *hesed,* "compassion."

A Hasid (plural, Hasidim) was a lover of God and godliness. Holy companies of Hasidim gathered around charismatic mystics called rebbes (masters; singular rebbe, pronounced reh-beh) or *tzaddikim* (saints; singular *tzaddik*). The role of the rebbe was to model the passionate love of God and godliness that was *d'veikus* and to mentor the Hasid in achieving it. Over time, the rebbe's role grew from mentor to intermediary. While the Baal Shem Tov taught that *d'veikus* was achievable by anyone, later teachers made it clear that the level of saintliness needed to achieve union with God was so high that only the *tzaddikim* could reach it. Their disciples could come close by drawing close to their rebbe. Focus shifted from God to the rebbe, and Hasidism began a slow decline.

The essential message and practice of early Hasidism are simple. The message: "*M'lo kol ha-aretz k'vodo,* the whole earth is full of God's glory" (Isaiah 6:3). The practice: "*Shiviti Adonai l'negdi tamid,* I place God before me always" (Psalm 16:8). Understand these and you understand Hasidism.

Despite originating in the Hebrew Bible, the message that the whole earth is filled with God—at least as the Hasidim understood it—led to the charge that Hasidism is Jewish pantheism, teaching that "all is God." This is incorrect. Pantheism identifies creation with the Creator: God and nature are synonymous. Hasidism teaches a philosophy rightly called panentheism: all is *in* God. This is a crucial difference. Where the world is God in pantheism, the world is only part of God in panentheism. That is, while God fills all the world, the world does not fill all of God. God embraces and transcends creation.

What is nonetheless quite radical in this teaching is the intimacy of God and creation. The early Rabbis, led by Rabbi Akiva (*Genesis Rabbah* 1:14), spoke of creation *ex nihilo:* God created the world out of nothing. "Before the world was created, the Holy One, Blessed be He, with His Name alone existed" (*Pirke d'Rabbi Eliezer* 10). How God did this is problematic, and much of Jewish theological speculation tries to explain just what creation out of nothing means.

Centuries later, the kabbalists, Jewish mystics, understood God to be *Ayn,* the No-thing that creates all things. For them, creation from nothing meant creation from No-thing, creation from God. God emanates creation the way the sun emanates rays of sunlight. Successive generations of kabbalists created more and more complex creation theories, culminating in the cosmology of Isaac Luria, the sixteenth-century Safed kabbalist known as the *Ari,* an acronym for "the Holy Rabbi Isaac."

Luria introduced the idea of *tzimtzum,* contraction. He taught that because God is *Ayn Sof,* the Unending Infinite, if there is to be a finite creation then God must first make room for finity. This God does through an act of self-contraction. God contracts from the center (imagine a bagel) and in that center hole creation happens.

According to Luria, God's act of *tzimtzum* was followed by a process of divine emanation: God pours Divine Light into vessels meant to contain it within the newly created emptiness at the center of God. The process failed, however. The vessels shattered, and most of the light returned to God. Some sparks of light became trapped in the shards of the broken vessels. God is now "in exile" from God.

One can see how this myth of an exiled God spoke so powerfully to the Jews, who themselves were in exile for sixteen hundred years, and who had just experienced a massive expulsion from Spain in 1492. Add to this Luria's teaching of *tikkun,* repair—that the reason for the Jewish exile was to bring about the end of God's exile by returning the lost sparks of Divine Light to their source—and the popularity of Lurianic theosophy is ensured. The Jew is God's chosen custodian, who, by scrupulously adhering to the mystical intentions of the commandments revealed by Luria and his disciples, engages the world in such a manner as to reclaim and return the lost sparks of God to their Source. Because these sparks are exiled throughout the earth, so the Jew must be exiled throughout the world. Exile is not a punishment for misdeeds but a necessary assignment promoting the process of *tikkun*, which will find completion in the future.

This essentially hopeful cosmology became normative after Luria's death in 1572. It also became very complicated. Although the means to *tikkun* was adherence to the *mitzvos*, each mitzvah had to be done with the proper *kavvanah*, or intention. Mastering the *kavvanot* (plural) became the province of a new elite, the scholar/mystic.

Hasidism never denied Luria's theology; it simply recast it in a radically new way. What for the kabbalist was a cosmological fact became for the Hasid a psychological truth. Can it be, asked Hasidism, that the Infinite can become finite? Of course not; the Infinite includes the finite and is not in opposition to it. Yet, if *Ayn Sof*, the Unbounded, sets boundaries—which is what Luria implies in the teaching of *tzimtzum*, divine contraction—that is precisely what happens. God cannot be God and be bounded. So is Luria wrong? No, not wrong, simply a bit off: What Luria said took place in God actually takes place in the human mind.

Our experience of God and creation is inherently dualistic: We see self and other, God and creation, good and evil, and all the myriad dyads that make up our view of reality. We project that dualism onto God, speaking in terms of contraction and expansion, brokenness and repair, exile and redemption. But that is all it is: a projection. God is *Ayn Sof*, without end, and is therefore an unbroken nonduality. *D'veikus*, union with God, is not something to be achieved but a given to be realized. The goal is not to effect *d'veikus* but to realize it, to experience *da'at d'veikus*, an awareness of God's nonduality present in, with, and as all things.

Lurianic Kabbalah became a complicated system of doing and thus fell under the control of a master class of advanced doers. Early Hasidism reclaimed *d'veikus* for the masses by teaching that it wasn't something you had to do but something you simply had to acknowledge. You didn't have to master hundreds of *kavvanot,* you had to master only one: an intense desire for God. If your heart is broken in its yearning for God, you will break through the very idea of brokenness and see that God was, is, and always will be whole.

Although the Hasidim themselves do not use this analogy, the relationship of a wave to the ocean aptly captures the situation Hasidism says we are in. Imagine yourself a self-conscious wave on the ocean. You look around you and see other waves. These differ from you in size, shape, and distance. Your sense of self is at least partly derived from comparing yourself with these other waves. And as you do you notice that some waves, those farther in front, crash against the rocks and disappear.

You look to see what happens to them, and it soon becomes clear to you that they no longer exist. More than that, you can see that their fate will soon be yours. To escape this meaningless destruction, you begin to imagine a way out. Perhaps there is another ocean after this one. Perhaps you will return to this ocean in another form. And on and on. What you never do is realize that you are the ocean, and the ocean is unaffected by the rise and fall of waves. The problem is not with the ocean and its waving, but with your misunderstanding of the nature of who and what you are. All that is required of you is to realize your true nature. You are the ocean in extension. When you crash against the rocks, your particular form disappears, but your true self, your oceanic self, stays the same. The problem is where you choose to focus your attention. Focus on yourself as a wave, and you are increasingly frantic and worried. Focus on yourself as the ocean, and you find tranquility and peace of mind. Lurianic Kabbalah tried to explain how the ocean waves; Hasidism tries to wake the wave up to being the ocean. Awakening to your true nature is what it is to "place God before you always." Everywhere you look you see God, not as an abstract spirit but as the True Being of all beings.

Cast of Rabbis ☐

These stories reflect actual events in the lives of real people. I have appended short biographical notes to each story, but I also thought it would be helpful to list them here as a group.

A word about gender. The rabbis listed here are all men. There were and are no women rabbis among the Hasidim. Although this may render these stories problematic for, and even irrelevant to, some readers, I hope you can see beyond it. I believe that the stories collected here are of great value despite their limitations of culture. The case of gender equality and inclusivity must be made strongly in our time, but do not let that need rob you of the genius of past times.

Aharon of Karlin (1736–1772): A Hasid of Rabbi Dov Ber of Mezritch, Reb Aharon introduced Hasidism to Lithuania, where the name "Karliner" became synonymous with "Hasidic." He is known for his ecstatic prayer, care for the needy, and focus on moral development.

Avigdor Halberstam (dates of birth and death unknown): Brother of Rabbi Chaim of Zanz, and rabbi of Dukla in Galicia.

Avraham haMalech (1739–1776): An ascetic who preferred solitude to public life, Avraham haMalech was the son of Dov Ber, the *Maggid* of Mezritch. Called *haMalach* (the Angel) due to his extreme asceticism, Avraham refused to succeed his father, preferring to focus on his own spiritual practice and allow others to take up the role of Hasidic rebbe.

Avraham of Parisov (dates of birth and death unknown).

Avraham Yaakov of Sadigora (1819–1883): The son of, and successor to, Rabbi Yisrael of Ruzhin.

Avraham Yehoshua Heschel of Apta (d. 1825): Famous for his ecstatic sermons, the Rav (senior rabbi) of Apta, as he was called, was also respected as a mediator between different Hasidic communities.

Baal Shem Tov (1698–1760): The founder of Hasidic Judaism, the Besht (acronym for Baal Shem Tov, "Master of the Good Name") was orphaned at an early age and raised as a ward of his village. Beginning in his early twenties, he devoted himself to mystical practices. At the age of thirty-six, he revealed himself as a healer, hence the title Baal Shem (Master of the Name) given to spiritual healers who used the Name of God in their healing work. The *tov,* "good," appended to his title reflected the quality of his character as well as his efficacy as a healer. The Besht believed that God was everywhere and could be found by anyone whose heart was open, simple, and pure. At a time when Judaism was focused on a scholar elite, he reached out to the masses with a Judaism rich in compassion, devotion, and hope. His inner circle of disciples took his teachings out into the larger world, creating a global movement that continues to this day.

Baruch, the Maggid of Rika (dates of birth and death unknown): A tutor of the children of Rabbi Levi Yitzchak of Berditchev.

Chaim (Halberstam) of Zanz (1793–1876): A noted scholar and Hasidic rebbe (master), Rabbi Chaim lived simply among his disciples in western Galicia, giving away most of his money to charity. His modest style of living clashed with that of the rebbes of Sadigora and Ruzhin, and he criticized them for what he considered to be their lavish lifestyle.

Chanoch Henich of Alexander (1798–1870): Unlike some rebbes who fostered their own centrality in the lives of their students, Rabbi Chanoch emphasized personal effort in spiritual matters, and he understood the rebbe's role to be that of a guide and mentor, not an intermediary between the Hasid and God.

David Chein (1850–1925): A rabbinic leader of Chernigov, Russia, Reb David moved to Jerusalem in 1925 and died shortly after his arrival.

David of Lelov (d. 1814): A Hasid of Rabbi Yaakov Yitzchak, the

Chozeh (Seer) of Lublin, Rabbi David was famous for his compassion toward human beings and his great love for animals.

Dov Ber of Lubavitch (1773–1827): The son of, and successor to, Rabbi Schneur Zalman of Liadi, the founder of HaBaD Hasidism (see Shneur Zalman of Liadi, p. xxxviii). Dov Ber sought to make his Hasidim self-sufficient by helping them establish agricultural settlements. He bought land in Hebron, Palestine, and established a HaBaD community there.

Dov Ber of Mezritch (1704 [?]–1772): Known as the *Maggid* (Preacher) of Mezritch, Dov Ber was a towering intellect who focused his efforts on an elite following, providing Hasidism with a strong philosophical base. He succeeded the Besht after the latter's death, and created the institution of rebbe, charismatic leaders of independent Hasidic communities.

Elimelech of Lyzhansk (1717–1786): A Hasid of Dov Ber, he traveled widely with his brother, Rabbi Zusya of Hanipoli, raising money to pay the ransom of Jews held hostage by local brigands and landlords.

Eliyahu of Viskit (dates of birth and death unknown): A Hasid of Menachem Mendel of Kotsk.

Fishel of Strikov (d. 1825): A Hasid of Dov Ber and Elimelech of Lyzhansk, Fishel was known for his great modesty and righteous personality.

Levi Yitzchak of Berditchev (1740 [?]–1810): One of the most famous and beloved of Dov Ber's Hasidim, Levi Yitzchak was famous for his ability to see the best in people and for his intimate relationship with God, whom he saw and experienced everywhere.

Meir of Premishlan (1780 [?]–1850): Famous for his humor and his intense devotion during prayer, Meir lived in great poverty and yet devoted himself to alleviating the poverty of others.

Menachem Mendel of Kotsk (1787–1859): Unlike many of his contemporaries, Rabbi Menachem Mendel was known for his sharp tongue and demanding ways. He held that the ego was the enemy of spirituality and must be removed from the center of one's life. He spent the last twenty years of his life in seclusion, focusing on his relentless quest for absolute truth.

Menachem Mendel of Lubavitch (1789–1866): The grandson of Reb Shneur Zalman of Liadi, the founder of HaBaD Hasidism (see Shneur Zalman of Liadi, p. xxxviii), Rabbi Menachen Mendel was the third rebbe (after his grandfather and father) of the HaBaD movement. He was called the *Tzemach Tzedek,* after the title of his most famous book, a collection of legal rulings and commentaries.

Menachem Mendel of Rimanov (d. 1815).

Menachem Mendel of Vitebsk (1730–1788): One of the first Hasidic rebbes, Menachem Mendel traveled to Lithuania to meet and hopefully make peace with the Gaon of Vilna, the leader of the Mitnagdim, the opponents of the Hasidim. The Gaon refused to see him. In 1777, Reb Menachem Mendel led three hundred Hasidim and their families to Safed. He eventually settled in Tiberias, where he established a Hasidic community.

Menachem Mendel of Vizhnitz (1830–1884): Becoming a rebbe at the age of twenty-four, Rabbi Menachem Mendel attracted a large following and focused his energies on raising funds for Jews living in *Eretz Yisrael,* the Land of Israel. He is famous as the author of *Tzemach Tzaddik,* published after his death by his son and successor, Rabbi Baruch.

Menachem Mendel of Vorki (1819–1868): Called the Silent Tzaddik for his use of silence as a teaching tool, Rabbi Menachem Mendel is the "Zen rebbe," famous for his insistence on three things: an upright bow, a silent shout, and a motionless dance.

Mordechai of Chernobyl (1770–1837): The son and successor of Reb Nachum of Chernobyl, Reb Mordechai abandoned the poverty and wandering of his father and established a wealthy Hasidic court for himself and his followers.

Mordechai HaKohen (1835–1911): A noted sage and authority on Jewish law, Mordechai HaKohen authored seven volumes of legal commentary and opinion.

Mordechai of Lechovitch (d. 1810): Famous for his passionate and ecstatic prayer, Rabbi Mordechai was also known for his charitable efforts on behalf of Jews living in *Eretz Yisrael,* the Land of Israel.

Mordechai of Neshchiz (1740–1880): People traveled great distances seeking this noted healer and philanthropist's help in matters of health, both physical and financial.

Moshe of Kobrin (d. 1858): The founder of the Kobrin Hasidic line, Reb Moshe was known for his deep humility, insisting until his death that he was unfit to be called rebbe.

Moshe Zvi of Savran (d. 1838): The leading scholar in Berditchev and an arch opponent of the followers of Reb Nachman of Breslov.

Nachman of Breslov (1772–1811): Grandson of the Baal Shem Tov (his mother, Feige, was the Besht's daughter), Reb Nachman was known from his youth for his solitary devotions, asceticism, and ecstatic worship. Rabbi Nachman focused on the never-ending need for moral self-cleansing, and he held that despair was the greatest enemy of faith. He introduced a new element to Hasidism, the folktale. Before Reb Nachman, the Hasidim had told stories about other rebbes. Nachman's tales were allegorical fables about princesses and heroes. Unlike other rebbes, Nachman left no successor, and to this day his Hasidim draw their inspiration from his teachings, which were collected and published by his senior student Reb Noson Sternhartz.

Nachum of Chernobyl (1730–1787): A disciple of the Baal Shem Tov and later of Dov Ber of Mezritch, Reb Nachum was a wandering preacher who spread the teachings of his teachers; he also solicited money for the ransom of Jews held captive by local landlords.

Naftali of Ropshitz (1760–1827): A student of Rabbi Yaakov Yitzchak, the Seer of Lublin, Reb Naftali was famous for his wit.

Pinchas of Korets (1726–1791): A student of the Baal Shem Tov, Rabbi Pinchas disagreed with Dov Ber's contemplative and often esoteric approach to Hasidism, noting that it tended to be beyond the reach of the average Jew. He preferred instead the power of ecstatic prayer and heartfelt beseeching of God.

Shalom of Belz (1779–1855): Founder of the Belz Hasidic dynasty in Galicia, Reb Shalom had thousands of followers who made his miracle working famous throughout the world. His teaching stressed the importance of Talmudic learning.

Shalom Dov Ber of Lubavitch (1860–1920): The fifth Lubavitcher Rebbe, Shalom Dov Ber established Hasidic *yeshivot* in Soviet Georgia, bringing Hasidism to non-Ashkenazi Jewry.

Shalom Shachna of Probisht (1766–1803).

Shlomo Leib of Linchna (d. 1843): A Hasid of both the Seer of Lublin and the Holy Jew, Shlomo Leib was famous for his rejection of money and his refusal to utter a single unnecessary word.

Shmelke of Nikilsburg (1726–1778): A Hasid of Dov Ber, Rabbi Shmelke focused his life and his teaching around the work of philanthropy.

Reb Shmuel of Lubavitch (1834–1882): The youngest son of Reb Menachem Mendel of Lubavitch, Reb Shmuel succeeded his father as rebbe and continued his work of defending the rights of the Jews in czarist Russia.

Shneur Zalman of Liadi (1745–1812): A Hasid of Dov Ber, Rabbi Shneur Zalman established the HaBaD school of Hasidism. An acronym for *Hokhmah* (wisdom), *Binah* (Understanding), and *Da'at* (Knowledge), HaBaD stresses intellectual prowess along with ecstatic prayer and contemplative practice. He is the author of the most complete work of Hasidic philosophy, the *Tanya*.

Simcha Bunem of Pshischah (1765–1827): Before becoming a Hasid, Rabbi Simcha Bunem was a pharmacist and businessman, traveling widely and speaking fluent German and Polish. He became a Hasid after meeting Yaakov Yitzchak of Lublin, devoting himself to teaching the importance of attaining the proper internal spiritual states before engaging in prayer or *mitzvos* (religious acts).

Uri of Strelisk (d. 1826): Uri was called the *Seraph*, or Fiery Angel, because of the intense devotional energy generated by his prayers.

Yaakov Aryeh of Radzymin (1792–1874): A Hasid of Reb Simcha Bunem, Yaakov Aryeh was a noted miracle worker who founded his own Hasidic dynasty.

Yaakov David of Koznitz (dates of birth and death unknown): The chief justice of the rabbinic court of Koznitz, Yaakov David was a senior student of Reb Shlomo Leib of Linchna.

Yaakov Shimshon of Kosov (dates of birth and death unknown): Yaakov Shimshon was the rabbinic leader of Kosov from 1854 to 1880, when he was succeeded by his son Moshe.

Yaakov Yitzchak of Lublin (1745–1815): Called the *Chozeh*, or Seer, of Lublin for his ability to see into the souls of those who came to see him, Rabbi Yaakov Yitzchak used this ability to heal the spirits of people, helping them both spiritually and financially. Unlike many rebbes who saw themselves restricted to matters of the spirit, he saw his role as caring for people in all matters. Although he established no Hasidic line of his own, he was the teacher of most of the rebbes of the generation that came after him.

Yaakov Yitzchak of Pshischah (1766–1813): The senior Hasid of Yaakov Yitchak of Lublin, Yaakov Yitchak of Pshischah came to be called Yid HaKodesh, the "Holy Jew," because of his passionate emphasis on moral self-improvement. Disagreements developed between him and his rebbe, and Yid HaKodesh set up his own Hasidic community but died shortly thereafter.

Yechiel Meir of Gostynin (1816–1888): Called Der Tilim Yid, or the "Psalms Jew," because of his conviction that the recitation of the Psalms could cure all ills, spiritual and otherwise, Yechiel Meir was famous for his simple lifestyle and his welcoming and compassionate manner.

Yisrael of Koznitz (1733–1814): Known for his kind, sweet, and persuasive preaching style, Rabbi Yisrael taught that it was the rebbe's role to see the good in even the most wicked person, and speak to that goodness as a means of helping the person improve morally and spiritually.

Yisrael of Ruzhin (1797–1850): The great-grandson of Dov Ber, the Maggid (Preacher) of Mezritch, Rabbi Yisrael was a handsome and charismatic rebbe with a large following and a lavish lifestyle.

Yisrael Yitzchak of Radoshitz (dates of birth and death unknown): Son of, and successor to, Rabbi Yissachar Dov of Radoshitz.

Yissachar Dov of Belz (1854–1926): A leader of Orthodox as well as Hasidic Jews, Rabbi Yissachar Dov was a staunch opponent of Zionism and religious innovation.

Yissachar Dov of Radoshitz (1765–1843): Known as the Sava Kaddisha, the "Holy Grandfather," Rabbi Yissachar Dov lived in poverty and served as a tutor to Jewish children.

Yitzchak Aizik of Homil (1780–1857): A Hasid of Shneur Zalman of Liadi and his son Dov Ber of Lubavitch. Offered the position of rebbe after Dov Ber of Lubavitch's death, he declined.

Yitzchak Luria (1534–1572): Creator of the kabbalistic system known by his name (Lurianic Kabbalah), Yitzchak Luria focused his teaching on four things: the withdrawal of God to make room for creation; the shattering of the divine vessels meant to hold the divine energy needed to make a perfect world; the trapping of sparks of this divine energy in the world following the shattering of the vessels; and the task of *tikkun,* returning the divine sparks to God by engaging the world in a deeply hallowing manner.

Yitzchak Meir of Mezhibuzh (d. 1855): Son of Rabbi Avraham Yehoshua Heschel of Apta, Rabbi Yitzchak Meir was the father of Rachel, who became famous for her mastery of Talmudic teaching.

Yitzchak of Vorki (1779–1848): His devotion to helping oppressed Jews earned Rabbi Yitzchak the title "Lover of Israel."

Zusya of Hanipoli (d. 1800): A Hasid of Dov Ber, the *Maggid* (Preacher) of Mezritch, Rabbi Zusya was famous for his mystical wanderings with his brother, Rabbi Elimelech of Lyzhansk. His simple and welcoming style drew a large number of disciples to him.

Zvi Hirsch of Rimanov (1778–1847): Zvi Hirsch was called the Beadle, the "Assistant," for his long years of service to his rebbe, Menachem Mendel of Rimanov.

Hasidic Tales

1 Rabbi Naftali Tzvi Horowitz (b. Linsk, Galicia [Poland], 1760).

2 *Yetzer harah:* People are born with two impulses: *yetzer harah,* the impulse toward evil, and *yetzer hatov,* the impulse toward good. The *yetzer harah* is not evil per se, but rather a proneness to evil when it is not properly balanced by the *yetzer hatov.* Hence Hillel's teaching: "If I am not for myself, who will be for me? But if I am only for myself, what am I?" (*Pirke Avot* 1:14). A more accurate translation of these two impulses, then, would be the "selfish impulse" and the "selfless impulse." The sages taught that without the *yetzer harah* a person would not build a home, marry, or raise a family, for these require a sense of self and self-fulfillment (*Bereshit Rabbah* 9:7). The former becomes "evil" only when it is allowed to function without the counterbalance of the latter. When we act solely for the self, evil is possible: business becomes exploitative, marriage becomes oppressive, and sex becomes abusive. When we act for both self and other, the *yetzer harah* is given direction; it follows the lead of the good and lends its energy to attaining the good.

3 Genesis 4:7.

@ Every door has its own dangers. Every moment you have to make a choice: which inclination will you follow—the *yetzer harah* or the *yetzer hatov?*

Or can you honor them both? The *yetzer harah* is honored when you honor the needs of self; the *yetzer hatov* is honored when you respect the rights of others. Can you find a way to balance self and other, and in this way honor both inclinations to be in the world in a manner that hallows the world?

☐ Distractions

Reb Naftali of Ropshitz[1] once caught his son Eliezer engaged in some great prank.

"It isn't my fault," the boy said. "It's God's fault. God gave me a *yetzer harah*,[2] whose only task is to talk me into doing these terrible things. Don't blame me, blame Him!"

Reb Naftali scowled, then smiled and said: "God has given you the *yetzer harah* to instruct you."

"Instruct me? What can I learn from this trickster?"

"Faithfulness and perseverance," Reb Naftali replied. "Look how diligently the *yetzer harah* goes about its business. It never gets bored or tired of doing what God created it to do—to seduce people to selfish acts. Now you should never tire of doing what God created you to do—defeat it."

Eliezer listened carefully as his father spoke. When Reb Naftali had finished, Eliezer said: "But you have forgotten a very important thing."

"And what is that?" Reb Naftali asked.

"The *yetzer harah* goes about its task without fail because the *yetzer harah* has no *yetzer harah* to distract it with thoughts of doing otherwise. With people it is different, for 'sin crouches at the door.'[3] Every time we open the door to a new experience, the *yetzer harah* is waiting at the entrance to trick us into doing something wrong."

1 Align our souls with God: The relationship between God and soul is analogous to that between the sun and its rays. We are the extension of God in time and space. How, then, can we be misaligned with God? Misalignment is a state of mind that arises when we forget our true relationship with God and act as if God were other.

2 Lift up the heavens: Can heaven fall that it need be "lifted up"? No. Heaven and earth, up and down, go with each other. What falls is a veil of ignorance that blinds us from seeing the truth. When the veil is lifted, it appears to us that heaven is lifted, but in fact it is as it always was.

3 *Mechilta:* An ancient rabbinic commentary on the Book of Exodus.

4 *HaShem:* The Name, *Yud-Hay-Vav-Hay*, the four-letter Name of God, which is said to convey the essence of the Divine. Unpronounceable both in fact and in theory, the letters are a word play on the Hebrew verb "to be." God is That Which Is, Was, and Will Be. God is not "a being" or even "the supreme being" but rather Being Itself.

5 Exodus 20:13.

6 Genesis 4:9.

7 In the Book of Exodus 3:14, God reveals the essence of divinity to Moses: *ehyeh asher ehyeh,* most often translated as "I AM what I AM." A more accurate Hebrew translation would be "I will be whatever I will be." In either case, the Hasidic understanding of the text is the same: God is all that is. God is all that is happening at every moment. God is I AM—not a being or even a supreme being, but Being Itself. That means God is Cain, Abel, you, and me. This is what Reb Avraham means when he speaks of each as being a keeper of the I AM; just as a wave is a "keeper of" the ocean in its particular place and time, so are you a keeper of God in your particular place and time. To realize this about yourself is to realize it about all beings. It is to achieve this realization that you were born and blessed with life.

☐ Why Are You Here?

Reb Avraham of Parisov told this story:

Once I was present when Reb Yaakov Aryeh of Radzymin visited Reb Menachem Mendel of Kotsk. As Reb Yaakov entered the room, the rebbe turned to his guest and shouted: "Yaakov! In a few words tell me: Why are there humans in this world?"

Without hesitation, Reb Yaakov said: "We come into this world to align our souls with God."[1]

The Kotsker exclaimed: "Nonsense! Why are we here? We are here to lift up the heavens!"[2]

Not content with either answer, Reb Avraham would add his own understanding, saying:

"In fact, both sages are correct. We humans are here to align with God and in so doing to uplift the heavens. We know this from the *Mechilta*,[3] which teaches that the first five of the Ten Commandments parallel the second five. Thus, 'I am *HaShem*'[4] goes with 'Do not murder.'[5] To kill a human being is to diminish our capacity to bring godliness into the world.

"Thus, when God asks Cain after Cain had murdered his brother, Abel, 'Where is Abel?' Cain answers, 'I do not know. Am I my brother's keeper?'[6] We should understand Cain to be saying, 'I did not know that my brother was a keeper of I AM,[7] God; I did not know that by killing my brother I was weakening the influence of the divine I AM in this world.'"

2 Genesis 6:9.

3 Exodus 32:4.

4 Genesis 6:9.

@ True spiritual work takes us to the very ends of our endurance. It exhausts all our resources, pushing us to the breaking point. For it is only when we are about to break down that we have the opportunity to break through.

☐ Know Your Path

A great scholar once visited his rebbe to ask for advice regarding a career change. The scholar was tired of teaching and envious of those who always seemed to have time to relax, smoke their pipes, and meditate on the kabbalistic mysteries of God and creation.

"Teaching is exhausting," he complained to himself. "All the hours of preparation, and then the classroom time, not to mention the never-ending questions of my students! No wonder I have neither the time nor the energy to partake of the pleasures these others seem to enjoy."

When he arrived at the rebbe's home, he found his teacher ill and in bed. Before he could greet his rebbe and wish him *refuah shelemah,*[1] the rebbe silenced him and said:

"Let me teach you the secret of the Torah's phrase 'These are the offspring of Noah.'[2] The word 'Noah' means 'easy' or 'convenient.' The word 'these' connects this sentence with another: 'These are your gods, O Israel.'[3] What is the connection? We tend to make idols out of the easy and to worship convenience rather than truth. There is no telling whose effort is greater or lesser. All we can say is whether or not our effort is true to ourselves."

The scholar nodded, awed that his teacher could read his thoughts. But he was not yet satisfied. "What you say is true, Rebbe, yet Torah also tells us 'Noah walked with God.'[4] What does this mean?"

(continued on page 9)

[e] This is what the rebbe knows and what the scholar has to learn. He is mistaking "Noah" for God, ease for reality. He is convinced that if he were to devote himself to some other career, he would have the leisure needed to awaken to the Presence of God. But his longing for God is being replaced by his longing for leisure. And when he gets it, he will discover that leisure is no more a way to God than scholarship. The way depends on the wayfarer, not the wayfarer on the way.

Each person is a unique expression of the infinite diversity of God. While it is true that all of us share the same goal of aligning with God and lifting the veil of ignorance that blinds us to the Divine Presence in, with, and as all things, the ways to accomplish this are as varied as the people who accomplish it. What is your way? And how do you know it is, in fact, your way?

One way we investigate the rightness of our path is to compare our way with the ways of others. But when we do this, we often fail to see the difficulty of others' paths and imagine that they go through life with ease. It is then that our focus shifts from the goal—God—to the ease of the means. We want to "walk with God" without breaking a sweat. It rarely works that way.

The rebbe said, "We each have our own personal path to God. Some through meditation, some through labor, some through scholarship. We always see another's path as easier than our own, not knowing the struggles it entails. But if you abandon your path for another, you will find yourself lost, for you will worship the path and not the goal. Stay with your scholarship, my son. Toil day and night to wrest the mysteries from the text and to share them with your students. This is your path. This is the way you walk with God."

The scholar nodded, turned, and began his journey home.

1 Forty days: According to Jewish tradition, forty days is the amount of time one needs to free oneself from unwanted habits and instill desired habits in their place.

2 Baal Shem Tov (1698–1760): Rabbi Israel ben Eliezer was the founder of Hasidism. He began his public teaching in 1734 and soon earned the title Baal Shem Tov, Master of the Good Name (of God). He was an authentic healer of hearts, minds, and souls.

3 *Tehillim:* Psalms.

℮ You are what you say. The quality of your speech reflects the quality of your soul. Idle speech is thoughtless chatter, suggesting a scattered mind. If you wish to improve the latter, improve the former. But this effort must include all the words you use. Whether written, signed, spoken, or sung, a word has the power to heal or to harm. The problem with the fellow in our story is that he made a distinction between prayer and speech. It is all words, and no word should be spoken without full attention.

The Baal Shem Tov taught that a person is born with a fixed number of words to speak; when they are spoken, the person dies. Imagine that this is true for you. Every word you speak brings you closer to death. The next time you are about to utter a word, ask yourself whether this word is worth dying for.

☐ Idle Speech

A man once came across a teaching that said if you refrain from idle conversation for forty days[1] you will receive divine inspiration. Thinking this to be a shortcut to God, he set his mind to the task with great diligence. Forty days passed, and not once did an idle word cross his lips. And yet, at the end of his struggle, no inspiration was granted him. Seeking an explanation, he traveled to the Baal Shem Tov.[2]

After listening to the man's story, the Baal Shem Tov asked, "Did you pray during those forty days?"

"What a question!" the man exclaimed. "Of course I prayed. Three times a day I prayed, just as we are commanded by God."

"I see," said the Baal Shem Tov. "And did you read any *Tehillim*?"[3]

"Again, such a question! I am a Jew, and therefore I read Psalms every day." And to emphasize his point the man rattled off the first verses of his favorite psalm. "Master," he continued after the recitation, "can it be that the teaching is wrong? Can it be that after forty days of prayer and psalms and abstaining from idle conversation one does not receive divine inspiration?"

"No," said the Baal Shem Tov. "The teaching is true. It was your practice that was faulty. I can tell from your recitation of the psalm that while you took care to uplift your conversations, you babbled your prayers. They became your idle speech. You purified your conversation with people and defiled your conversation with God. Your prayers themselves kept you from receiving inspiration from God."

1 Days of Awe: The ten days from Rosh Hashanah to Yom Kippur, New Year's Day to the Day of Atonement, are devoted to deep self-reflection and repentance.

2 *Bat Kol* (literally, "Daughter of a Voice"): The Voice of God.

3 *Alef-beis:* The Hebrew *alef-bet,* or alphabet.

4 *Ribbono shel Olam:* Master of the Universe, one of the names of God.

5 *Alef, beis, gimmel…:* The first ten letters of the Hebrew alphabet.

@ Like a babbling baby, the scat of a jazz vocalist, or the *niggunim* (wordless melodies) of the Hasidim, the repetition of pure sound can open us to a world beyond words and the limited mindset that worships them. To repeat the letters over and again, to simply give voice to sound without locking it into fixed and conventional meanings, is to move from map to territory, from thoughts about God to God Itself. But the repetition cannot be done as technique. It must come from a profound realization that there is no technique. Like the fellow in our story, you have to become spiritually illiterate. Simply offer the sounds as sounds, and let God do the rest. Anything else is still an attempt to control the territory by manipulating the map.

☐ Ten Letters

Once, during the Days of Awe[1], the sainted kabbalist Yitzchak Luria heard a *Bat Kol*[2] telling him that for all his prayerful intensity there was one man in a neighboring town whose capacity for prayer exceeded even his own. As soon as he could, Reb Yitzchak traveled to that town and sought the man out.

"I have heard wondrous things regarding you," he said to the man when he found him. "Are you a Torah scholar?"

"No," the man said, "I have never had the opportunity to study."

"Then you must be a master of Psalms, a devotional genius who prays with great intensity."

"No," the man said. "I have heard the Psalms many times, of course, but I do not know even one well enough to recite it."

"And yet," Rabbi Luria cried, "I was told that the quality of your prayer surpasses even my own! What did you do during the Days of Awe that would merit such praise?"

"Rabbi," the man said, "I am illiterate. Of the twenty-two letters of the *alef-beis*[3] I know but ten. When I entered the synagogue and saw the congregation so fervent in their prayers, my heart shattered within me. I couldn't pray at all. So I said: *Ribbono shel Olam,*[4] here are the letters I know: *aleph, beis, gimmel, daled, hay, vav, zayin, chet, tes, yud.*[5] Combine them in a manner You understand, and I hope they will be pleasing to You. And then I repeated these ten letters over and over again, trusting God to weave them into words."

1 *Chumash* (from *chamesh,* "five"): The Torah, the Five Books of Moses.

2 Besht: An acronym of Baal Shem Tov, used lovingly to refer to Rabbi Israel ben Eliezer.

3 *Tzaddikim* (literally, "the Righteous Ones"): Mystic saints and holy masters.

4 *Torah lishmah:* Torah "for its own sake." Something done *lishmah* is something done without ulterior motive. *Torah lishmah* is the study of Torah for no other reason than the pure joy of honoring the text with our loving attention.

5 *Tzaddik:* Singular of *tzaddikim.*

@ Many people study the Bible, but few do so *lishmah.* Most people want something from the Bible: rules, truth, meaning, answers, clues to the past, prophecies of the future.

If you take up Torah with some goal in mind, it will reflect only your own desires. But if you look into it without desire, and allow the pure Light of God to penetrate your consciousness, you will see what God sees: a world of love and delight, and a way to live rooted in justice, compassion, humility, and peace.

☐ Light

A delegation of sages from a distant town visited the Baal Shem Tov on a matter of great urgency. He listened to their plight and then opened a *Chumash*[1] that was lying on the table before him. He looked at the text for a moment, closed the book, and then proceeded to tell his visitors not only how to handle their situation but also exactly what would transpire over the next few months to resolve their problem.

Over those months the events transpired just as the Besht[2] had predicted. The sages returned to the Baal Shem Tov to thank him for his insight and counsel. One among them asked, "Tell me, Master, is it by opening the Torah and looking inside it that you can perceive what is to happen and how best to respond to it?"

The Baal Shem Tov said: "We are taught that God created the world with light, and that this light illumined the world from one end to the other. Here and there, yesterday and tomorrow, were all present in the immediacy of that light. And God saw that the world was not worthy of this light, that access to it by the unscrupulous would cause global disaster, so God hid the light for the *tzaddikim*[3] to come, those few who could use it properly. Where did God hide this light? In the Torah. When a person peers into *Torah lishmah*,[4] for its sake and with no selfish motive, then a path is lit up, and past and future, time and space, are open in the moment. The *tzaddik*[5] sees the world as God sees the world: a creation of light."

1   *Shabbos:* Shabbat, the seventh day of the week.

2   Satan: The Hebrew word *satan* (pronounced *sah-tahn*) means "adversary." In later books of the Bible, Satan becomes a person, God's "prosecuting attorney."

3   Elijah: A ninth-century-B.C.E. prophet who avoided death and rose to heaven in a fiery chariot (2 Kings 2). In rabbinic lore, Elijah returns to earth to help people in need.

4   Carrying things outside the home on the Sabbath is considered work and therefore violates the prohibitions against working on the Sabbath.

5   In Exodus 16:25, Moses instructs the people regarding Sabbath meals. He uses the word "today" three times, which led to eating three Sabbath meals: Friday evening, Saturday noon, and a late afternoon meal called *Shalosh Seudos,* or *Seuda Shlishit,* the Third Meal.

6   *Melaveh Malkah* ("accompanying the Queen"): A celebratory meal at the conclusion of the Sabbath ushering the Sabbath Queen back to heaven until the following Sabbath.

☐ Hospitality

The parents of the Baal Shem Tov were famous for their hospitality. Each *Shabbos*[1] they would find poor travelers with no place to stay and welcome them into their home for the Sabbath. They would feed them and house them, and, when *Shabbos* ended, give them money and food for their travels. God took note of them and their generosity, and as often happens when God takes note of us, so, too, did Satan, the Accuser.[2]

God wished to bless these people with a child, but Satan desired to test their hospitality to see whether in fact they gave freely, or if in their hearts they harbored a hope of some heavenly reward. Sensing that Satan would not only test the couple but actively seek to trap them, Elijah the Prophet[3] offered to go in his stead. God agreed, and the following *Shabbos* Elijah returned to earth.

Disguised as a beggar and carrying a staff and knapsack in violation of the Sabbath,[4] Elijah knocked on the couple's door that *Shabbos* afternoon. Reb Eliezer opened the door, and the beggar pushed him aside and entered his home. "Good *Shabbos*," he said. "I am hungry and in need of shelter!"

Reb Eliezer welcomed the beggar, and his wife served him the Third Meal of the Sabbath.[5] The man ate and rested. He gave no thanks to either his hosts or his Maker. In the evening when *Shabbos* had ended, the couple prepared the *Melaveh Malkah*[6] for him. Again the man ate without any sign of gratitude. He spent the night in their home, and in the morning he was given food and sufficient money to see to his welfare. At that moment the beggar revealed himself to be Elijah the Prophet.

(continued on page 19)

☙ What is it about opening our door to strangers that makes this a central spiritual quality? The Torah tells us to love our neighbor only once (Leviticus 19:18) but urges us to love the stranger more than thirty times! Why? Hospitality requires that we step beyond the dualistic thinking of self and other, us and them. You open your door only after you have opened your heart. Hospitality is then an accurate reflection of the quality of your spirituality.

One who loves God but fears the stranger is one who doesn't understand God at all. God is the Other manifest in all others. The Besht's parents saw God manifest in every stranger and thus were no longer strangers to God. Loving God and loving the stranger are not two different things, but two different ways of honoring the same thing: the insight that all is God. Their intimacy with God translated into intimacy between themselves, which in turn gave birth to the Baal Shem Tov, who showed the world the One in whom all others dwell.

"I came to test your hospitality," the Prophet said, "to see the quality of your giving. And because you were gracious to me and never once commented on my insulting behavior, nor shamed me in any way, you have passed my test. God is pleased with my findings and finds you worthy of a son who will illumine the eyes of all Israel." That son was the Baal Shem Tov.

1 Hospitality is a central tenet of Judaism: "Let your home be wide open, and treat the poor like members of your household" (*Avot* 1:5). The sages of the Talmud list hospitality as among those acts "whose fruit is eaten in this world, and whose principle remains for the World to Come" (*Shabbat* 127a).

2 Torah (from the Hebrew root *yaroh*, "to teach"): Best understood as "teaching" or "instruction." The notion that Torah is primarily a legal code is false and misleading. It is a book of teaching about life and how best to live it, and it contains law but is not limited to law. Technically, Torah refers to the Five Books of Moses, but it is commonly used to refer to the entire body of Jewish teaching.

☐ Deeds Not Words

One winter a delegation of scholars visited the rabbi of Viedislav, the father of then five-year-old Simcha Bunem. The rabbi prepared a meal for his guests and, as they were eating, called to his son: "Simcha, go and prepare some new interpretation of the laws of hospitality[1] that you can share with our learned guests."

The boy left the table and returned a few minutes later. Everyone was surprised at his quick return. True, Simcha Bunem was a child prodigy when it came to Torah,[2] but even he should have taken longer to come up with a new and innovative interpretation of hospitality. Still, his father welcomed him back and said, "So, have you found a new interpretation of Torah?"

Simcha said that he had and that he would be happy to share it after his father's guests finished eating. When the meal was done, his father invited him to share his insights.

"I have nothing to say, father, but rather something to show."

Expecting a novel interpretation of law, both father and guests were perplexed. Seeing that the men remained seated, Simcha said, "Come and I will show you."

The entire delegation followed Simcha into another room of the house, and there they found his interpretation of hospitality: Simcha had prepared a bed for each guest complete with pillows and quilts folded neatly in place.

(continued on page 23)

@ The Hasidim speak of the Three Garments of the Soul, three ways in which the Divine enters into the world. We encounter these garments as thought, word, and deed, and we experience them as a cascade: thought leads to words, and words lead to deeds. The quality of each garment depends on the cleanliness of the one preceding it. Thus, we can see that everything depends on the quality of our thoughts.

When you were born, all three garments accompanied you into the world. Originally clean and free of the stain of selfishness, over time they become soiled and need refining. What soils them is selfishness. You begin to think only of yourself, speak only of your needs, and act in ways that exploit others in order to fulfill those needs. Cleansing the Garments of the Soul is the goal of spiritual practice.

But where to start? Because thought is key, you might expect to begin with that. But to think thought clean is like washing a windowpane with muddy water; this only smears the dirt but doesn't remove it. The way to cleanse thought is not to think but to do. This is what Simcha Bunem knew instinctively, and what we must know as well. If you wish to know God, begin by doing godly.

"And where, little one, is the novelty in your interpretation?" one of the rabbis asked.

"With all due respect, Teacher," Simcha Bunem said, "if I had simply provided you with a new set of words you would have a chance to rest only your minds, but in this way I offer you a chance to rest your bodies as well."

1 Levi Yitzchak (1740–1810): The most beloved Hasidic rebbe after the Baal Shem Tov, Levi Yitzchak was persecuted by the enemies of Hasidism and was forced to resign from several rabbinic posts before becoming the rebbe of Berditchev in Russia. His main teaching focused on humility. No matter what our achievements, we are as nothing before the majesty of God. Humility comes when we reflect on God's infinite Presence in, with, and as all things.

2 Sodom and Amora: Sodom and Gomorra, legendary cities that were destroyed by God because of the violence, selfishness, and greed of their citizens.

@ Being kind, generous, just, and holy is not convenient. It requires attention, self-restraint, and great discipline. Why? Because our instinct is not for holiness but for self-preservation. Our reptilian brain comes with a single set of encoded instructions: eat or be eaten; kill or be killed. This is not a moral judgment; there is no morality at the level of the reptilian brain. It is simply an observation. Morality comes with the neocortex, the higher brain, and to impose morality on the lower brain is as difficult and as dangerous as wrestling an alligator. Just as an alligator squirms to slip out of our arms, so the reptilian brain twists and turns to convince us that feeding its endless hungers is just and good.

And sometimes it works. We pass selfish laws draped in the trappings of compassion. We do this as a people, and we do this as individuals. Rebbe Levi Yitzchak knew this, and he made it clear to the legislators of Berditchev. To their credit, they saw the truth of his insight and did not pass their law. But what about you? You are also law abiding. You also make rules that govern your behavior and to which you can point to attest to your piety and righteousness. But is it true? Are these good laws, or just clever excuses for selfishness?

Whenever you are about to make another law for yourself, ask Levi Yitzchak to join the conversation. Ask him to judge whether this new law is for the welfare of others or simply to serve the needs of the self.

☐ Seeking a Precedent

When Reb Levi Yitzchak[1] was asked to be the rabbi of Berditchev, he agreed on one condition: that the local leadership not draw him into their communal disputations unless they were about to make a new law.

Several months later, the leaders asked the rebbe to attend a town council. When he arrived, the council leader welcomed him. "We are honored by your presence, Rebbe, and in need of your advice. We are deliberating a new law making it illegal for the poor to knock on the doors of householders to request alms. Instead, they will be aided monthly from a newly formed community chest."

The elder stopped and waited for the rebbe to speak. He expected to wait some time, as the council itself had taken months to come to this decision, but instead Reb Levi Yitzchak spoke up immediately.

"It was my understanding," the rebbe said, "that you are to invite me to these meetings only if you are considering creating new laws— laws without precedent. This case certainly doesn't meet that requirement."

Startled, the elder said: "Rebbe, this is indeed just such a law. There is no precedent for this procedure."

Reb Levi Yitzchak shook his head sadly. "My friends, you are mistaken. This law can be traced all the way back to Sodom and Amora,[2] for they too had a law that let people escape their responsibility to the poor."

The council voted down the proposal then and there.

1 Hasidim: Disciples of Hasidic masters. The word *Hasid* comes from the Hebrew *chesed,* "compassion." Hasidism is the way of compassion rooted in the experience of God as the source and substance of all beings. Hasidim are the students of compassion, seeking to experience God and live out godliness.

2 *Kashrut:* The laws of kosher. Kosher (Hebrew, *kasher*) means "fit" or "proper" for human consumption according to the biblical and rabbinic dietary codes.

3 *Shochet:* A person trained in the art of kosher slaughtering, being able to take the life of an animal in a manner that minimizes the animal's suffering.

@ The Baal Shem Tov taught that every word you overhear, no matter how seemingly inconsequential, is in fact spoken for your ears alone.

Every moment, life presents you with another opportunity to look within yourself and see where you can improve the quality of your thought, word, and deed. Do not imagine that the world revolves around you—it doesn't. But know that whatever is in the world is in you as well. Let reality be your rebbe.

☐ A Kosher Tongue

Reb Yaakov Yitzchak of Pshischah, the Yid HaKodesh, once ordered his senior disciple, Reb Simcha Bunem, to make a journey to a distant hamlet. When he inquired as to the purpose of the journey, the Yid HaKodesh remained silent.

Reb Simcha Bunem took several hasidim[1] with him and left on the journey. The sky had already turned to dusk by the time they arrived at their destination. Because the town had no inn, Reb Simcha Bunem ordered his coachman to stop at the first cottage. He knocked at the door and was invited in along with his students. When they asked whether they could join their host for dinner, the man replied that he had no dairy food and could offer them only a meat meal.

Instantly, the Hasidim bombarded the man with questions about his level of *kashrut*.[2] Who was the *shochet*?[3] they demanded to know. Were the animal's lungs free of even the smallest blemish, and was the meat salted sufficiently to draw out all traces of blood, as was required by law? The interrogation would have continued had not a commanding voice from the back of the cottage called out to them.

They turned their attention from the owner of the home to a man dressed as a beggar sitting near the hearth smoking a pipe. "My dear Hasidim," the beggar said. "With regard to what goes into your mouths, you are scrupulous. Yet, regarding what comes out of your mouths, you make no inquiries at all!"

When Reb Simcha Bunem heard these words, he knew the reason for this journey. He nodded respectfully to the beggar, thanked the householder for his concern, and returned to the wagon, saying to his students, "Come, we are now ready to return to Pshischah."

1 *Gan Eden:* Garden of Eden.

2 *Gut in Himmel:* "God in heaven!" a common Yiddish expression of awe.

3 *Ribbono shel Olam:* Master of the Universe, considered an intimate name for God.

4 *HaShem:* The Name. The Name of God, made up of four Hebrew consonants, YHVH, is unpronounceable according to both Jewish law and the limits of human speech. The euphemism HaShem, or The Name, is used to refer to this Name of God.

🄴 What do you have by which to honor another? Your mind? Your heart? Your skill? All of these are gifted to you by God. The thoughts you think and the ideas you nurture can all be traced to teachers and sages of the past. The feelings you feel are not yours; you cannot keep the ones you like and discard the ones you dislike. The works of your hands are the result of tutoring and mentoring by others. All you have and all you are come to you from the efforts of others and, ultimately, the grace of God. Without these gifts you have nothing; indeed, without them you are nothing.

When you realize you are nothing without the constant gifting of God and the universe, you realize you have nothing to offer another and must rely solely on God. *"Ribbono shel Olam,* I am nothing without You and the gifts with which You grace my life. I cannot honor another and can only turn to You. Use me as a vehicle for the blessings of others, and I shall be grateful for the opportunity to serve." When you can pray these words with sincerity, you are ready to taste the spice of *Gan Eden.*

☐ A Recipe from Heaven

On a journey to visit the *Chozeh* of Lublin, Reb David of Lelov stopped at the home of a dear friend with whom he hoped to make the rest of the journey. His friend was quite poor, yet he asked his wife to prepare a meal for his beloved David.

The woman was shocked. All she had was a bit of flour, not even a pinch of salt or a drop of oil to add a bit of flavor. Still, she went out to the forest, gathered twigs for a fire, mixed her flour with water, and boiled dumplings for her husband, their friend, and herself.

When Reb David returned home from Lublin, he told his wife of his journey. "When I ate with my friend, his wife prepared a meal of such delicacy that it tasted as if it was flavored with spice from *Gan Eden*.[1] Never have I eaten such food!"

Knowing her husband to be of a mystical bent and unimpressed by things of this world, Reb David's wife knew that this delicacy must be rare indeed. She set off at once for the friend's house and asked his wife to share the recipe with her.

"What delicacy?" she said. "It was flour and water."

"No, no," the other insisted. "My David said it tasted like something from *Gan Eden!*"

Suddenly her friend's eyes grew wide with astonishment. "*Gut in Himmel!*"[2] she said. "When I was gathering the twigs for the fire, I prayed to God, saying, '*Ribbono shel Olam*,[3] I have nothing with which to honor Reb David, but You, *HaShem*,[4] You have the Garden of Eden. So please, won't You add a bit of spice to these dumplings I am cooking that Reb David might find some enjoyment in them?' It seems that *HaShem* heard my prayer!"

1 *Lamed Vavnik:* Hidden Saint, from the Hebrew letters *lamed* and *vav*, whose numerical value equals thirty-six. A *Lamed Vavnik* is a saint who works selflessly behind the scenes to see that goodness triumphs over evil. There are thought to be thirty-six Hidden Saints in the world at all times, and it is by the goodness of their deeds that the world survives.

2 Kabbalah (from the Hebrew *kabel*, to receive): Jewish mystical tradition. Midnight was considered a moment outside normal time. Studying at midnight allowed the kabbalist to slip the bonds of normal consciousness and enter paradise.

3 *Tzedakah* (from *tzedek*, justice): The act of donating 10 percent of one's earnings to the poor.

4 *Tzaddik* (from *tzedek*, justice): A saint.

@ Acts of generosity are essential to the spiritual life, reflecting as they do an awareness of the interconnectedness of all beings. Judaism sets a minimum standard for giving: ten percent of your earnings. But the Hasid, the compassionate disciple of God, goes beyond the letter of the law. Reb Shalom gave of his losses also.

You may not aspire to such a level of sainthood, but your connection with others is no less than that of Reb Shalom. The question is: How generous are you? Do you even meet the minimum standard of *tzedakah*, or are you apt to give less in the hope of having more? The next time you wonder how far you are progressing on the spiritual path, don't look only to the sacred books on your shelf, but look also to the checkbook in your drawer or purse.

☐ A Hidden Tzaddik

It was common for great rabbis to come from lines of great rabbis. Rabbi Mordechai HaKohen was once asked about his grandfather, Reb Shalom, of whom no one had ever heard. Rabbi Mordechai said: "Truly he was a *Lamed Vavnik*, a Hidden Saint.[1] By day he would earn his living as a goldsmith, all the while focusing his mind on the deepest mysteries of the Torah. And at night he would arise at midnight to study the words of Kabbalah.[2] And not only this," Rabbi Mordechai continued, "as was customary among all the pious, my grandfather would set aside a tenth of his earnings for the poor."

The questioner said: "With all due respect, Rabbi, this is not so unusual. Many of us meditate on Torah during the day and study Kabbalah at night. And every Jew is obligated to give a tenth of all earnings to see to the welfare of the poor."

Rabbi Mordechai smiled. "So there is more," he said. "My grandfather would give a tenth of his profits to *tzedakah*,[3] and he would give a tenth of his losses as well."

"I am not sure I understand," the other said.

"My grandfather once lost a lot of money when he failed to refine a great amount of gold properly. He calculated one tenth of this loss and took that amount out of his savings and gave it to the poor."

"But we are required to share only our profits, not our losses, for to do otherwise would compound those losses."

"Which is why my grandfather was a *tzaddik*.[4] He believed we are to bless God for all that comes to us, the bad as well as the good. And he believed that the poor should not suffer from his own mistakes. Therefore, my grandfather chose to give thanks to God for his losses as well as his earnings by donating ten percent of each to the poor."

1 Psalm 104:1.

☐ The Successor

The Baal Shem Tov did not appoint anyone to take his place when he died. Instead, he instructed his Hasidim to seek out his successor among the teachers of his day.

"But how will we recognize him?" his disciples asked.

"You will ask him this question," the Besht said. "How might one be rid of conceit?"

"And if he knows the answer, he is our teacher?"

"On the contrary," the Baal Shem Tov said. "Anyone who claims to know how to be free of conceit is a liar. Conceit comes with having a sense of self, and the self cannot get rid of itself. And thinking otherwise is the height of conceit."

"Yet," one Hasid said, "is it not true that we are created in the image of God? Do we not reflect the Divine within ourselves? God is not filled with conceit, so how can we be?"

The Baal Shem Tov replied, "In Psalms we read: 'God reigns clothed with majesty.'[1] God's 'majesty' is in fact humility, and the Infinite God wears robes of infinite humility. Now it is true that humans mirror God, but just as a mirror reverses what it reflects, so the human world often reverses the godly. Thus, if the humility of God is infinite, the hubris of humanity is no less so."

(continued on page 35)

ⓔ   What does it mean that the majesty of God is in fact the humility of God? The word "majesty" suggests a glorious presence: the majesty of a king or a queen is not hidden but honored; the majesty of a sunset is so powerful as to take one's breath away. Can the majesty of God be so different from these?

Yes, indeed. Because our world mirrors God and thus often reverses godliness, we imagine God's greatness to be over and above us when in fact it is below and beneath us. Genesis 1:2 tells us that God hovered over the waters—and where do the waters dwell except in the low places? God is not the powerful king lording it over us from on high; God is the subtle guide supporting us from below.

When we imagine God on high, we assume that spiritual practice is a struggle to climb the tallest mountain peaks by sheer force of will. Yet, when we discover God in the lowest of places, spiritual practice is a simple surrender to gravity: It is effortless and natural. It is also humbling. Where is the victory in sliding down the mountain? Where is the pride in surrender? There is no victory or pride, and that is the Baal Shem Tov's point. A rebbe who claims to have mastered conceit is an ego still climbing, hoping to place its flag on the summit. A rebbe who knows this conceit and realizes the improbability of escape from it is ready to surrender to the fact that you cannot get to God, you can only give in to God.

When the Baal Shem Tov died and the time of mourning had passed, his senior students went out in search of his successor. They spoke to many great teachers and saints, and from each one they inquired how they might remove conceit from their hearts. Each *tzaddik* offered words of wise counsel. Finally, they came to Reb Pinchas of Korets and posed their question.

The *tzaddik* shook his head and said, "I, too, stand in fear of this, and I know of no way out."

"This one," the Hasidim said, "is our new rebbe."

1 Rebbe: Hasidic master.

2 *Shabbos:* The Sabbath.

3 *Niggunim:* Wordless melodies. The Hasidic masters taught that song and dance could uplift the soul, and that every melody, no matter how secular, contained a spark of divinity that could be released if sung with the right intention. The Hasidic masters created their own *niggunim* as direct gateways to God.

4 *Tish:* A special meal hosted by the rebbe in which Hasidim gather to eat, drink, sing, and study.

☐ You Are What You Think

It is the habit among Hasidim to gather with their rebbe[1] on the afternoon of Shabbos[2] and share food, schnapps, niggunim,[3] and some words of Torah. One Shabbos at the tish[4] of Reb Moshe of Kobrin, so many Hasidim arrived that scores of them could not find room at the table. They crowded around the feast, eager to taste a bit of food, catch a glimpse of their rebbe, and hear a word of Torah.

Despite the crowd, Reb Moshe noticed a fellow standing in a corner. Reb Moshe called to his attendant. "Who is that young man standing over there?" he asked. When he heard the Hasid's name, he said, "I don't know him."

"But Rebbe, you must recognize him," his attendant said. "He is a pious fellow, who comes often to your table. You have spoken to him on many occasions." The attendant proceeded to remind the rebbe of the young man, his parents, and several incidents that the attendant thought might rekindle the rebbe's memory.

Finally, Reb Moshe called the man to his side. "I have been trying to remember who you are and have had a very hard time doing so. Just now I realized what the problem is.

(continued on page 39)

37

@ You are what you think; so what are you thinking about right now? There are two basic thoughts reflecting our twofold nature. You are born with two inclinations: the *yetzer hatov* and the *yetzer harah*. The first leads you toward love, moving you beyond yourself to the world. The second leads you toward fear, moving you away from the world into yourself. These two inclinations give rise to two fundamental categories of thought: love and fear. When your thoughts come from love, you think about caring for self and other. When your thoughts come from fear, you think about only yourself. When you think about only yourself, you are consumed by hunger: hunger for safety, for surety, for security. And because there is no safety, surety, or security in the isolated ego, your hungers are never satisfied. You eat and eat and eat and never become full.

The Rabbis teach that heaven and hell each consists of identical banquets of the finest foods. People sit around the table with forks and spoons six feet in length, far too long to be useful for feeding oneself. In hell, each guest starves. In heaven, each learns to feed the person across the table, and all are full.

The challenge is not to get rid of your hunger but to satisfy the hunger of another and in this way to be fed yourself.

"You see, the essence of a person is found in his thoughts. Wherever you focus your mind, that is who you are. All this time I have been watching you, and your mind has been wandering from one desire to another. First you hungered for this; then you hungered for that. There was no end to your cravings. All I could see was this incessant hunger. As long as I did so, I could not tell whether you were a man who happened to have a mouth, or a mouth masquerading as a man."

The young Hasid was embarrassed to have had his thoughts read by his rebbe. From that day forth he did his best to focus his thinking on holy things.

@ How much time do you spend trying to scare away your own reflection? For many, if not most of us, this can be a full-time job. We look at the world as a pie of fixed size, and then find ourselves in competition with everyone else for a bigger and bigger slice. What determines our competitive approach is our assumption that the pie is fixed. This is called a zero-sum game: If you are to win, everyone else must lose.

But what if the pie is infinite? What if there is plenty for everyone if we would just stop trying to grab and hoard? If this were true, we wouldn't be fearful or jealous of others; we wouldn't assume that someone else's success is always at our expense. Yet, it might still be true that others have more than us.

Reb Meir is not talking about "abundance thinking." He is not advocating "think and grow rich" strategies. He is simply saying that we are not in charge of our own success. God is in charge; reality will determine your success or failure. All you can do is all you can do. You can make sure your product or service is sound. You can make sure your business practices are ethical. You can make sure your presentation is persuasive. But in the end, you cannot guarantee your own success. You are not in charge of the results; all you can do is maximize the chance of success. Or maximize the chance of failure.

What is the advantage of surrendering the results to God? You get to focus on what you can control: the quality of your own effort. In the end it is this, not any imagined payoff, that will bring you a sense of joy, purpose, and peace.

☐ Horse Sense

A fellow once came to ask the advice of Reb Meir of Premishlan. He complained bitterly that a competitor was robbing him of his livelihood.

"Have you ever noticed that when a horse goes to the river to drink, it strikes its hoof against the bank? Do you know why it does this?"

The man just stared at the rebbe, angry that he seemed to have missed the whole point of his complaint.

"I will tell you why," the rebbe said. "When the horse bends its head close to the river to drink, it sees its face reflected in the water. Mistaking the reflection for another horse, it stomps on the ground to scare the other away and preserve the water for itself.

"Now, you and I find such behavior silly. We know that the horse's fear is groundless, and that the river is capable of watering far more horses than just this one."

"And what does this stupid horse have to do with me and my livelihood?"

"You, my friend, are this horse. You imagine that the river of God's bounty cannot sustain both you and another, so here you are stomping your hooves to scare away an imagined competitor."

"Imagined?" the man said.

"God has set the wealth of each of us, and no one can subtract from what God has set aside. Run your business as wisely as you can, and know that whatever comes to you is decreed in heaven. Your only true competition is the reflection of self you see in the river."

1 *Nebbich:* Yiddish for a foolish person, a loser.

ⓔ Humility is highly valued among the Hasidim as a sign of spiritual maturity. But what is true humility? This story presents us with three approaches to humility. The first is the false humility of Reb Moshe's wondering aloud whether it is the carriage or the horses that the people are honoring and not himself. Although this may fool his devout Hasid, we are not taken in. He knows they are coming out to honor him and not his horse.

The second is a more virulent false humility, which causes Reb Moshe to vomit. His stomach turns because he is convinced that he does not deserve such honor. He is obsessed with his own unworthiness, but the mere fact of his obsession suggests that his focus is fundamentally selfish and vain. This is clearly a Shakespearean case of "the man doth protest too much."

The third approach to humility is that taught by Reb Yisrael: When honors come, accept them calmly. And when they pass, allow them to pass calmly. Do not place any importance on them, and do not place any unimportance on them. They are like rain: They come and they go, and there is no need to make a fuss about it.

Not making a fuss may well be a truer sign of spiritual maturity than that of humility. Those who crave the adulation of others and those who shun it are both trapped in their own drama. Better to allow reality simply to unfold as it will, and not pretend that we have much to say about it one way or the other.

☐ Receive and Detach

Once, Reb Yisrael of Ruzhin listened to a Hasid of Reb Moshe Zvi of Savran extol the virtues of his teacher.

"Reb Moshe is a man of deep humility," the Hasid said. "Even the slightest sign of honor given to him would make him question his own worth. He never thought he was worthy."

The Hasid paused, expecting a comment from Reb Yisrael marveling at the humility of his master. Reb Yisrael said nothing, and the Hasid continued:

"Indeed, there is one town so taken with my rebbe that whenever he visits, the whole town turns out to honor him."

"And this troubles him?" Reb Yisrael asked.

"Troubles him, indeed! First he would say it was the carriage they honored, noting its fine construction. Then he would hope it was the horses they honored, marveling at their strength. But in the end he knew it was him they honored. He would worry over the vanity of humankind to the point of making himself sick. He would actually vomit from all the fuss made over him!"

"*Nebbich!*"[1] Reb Yisrael exclaimed. "This poor fellow! Could he not find a better way to deal with honor than to vomit? There is a simple method: to receive all honor and yet to be attached to none of it. It wasn't the honor that caused our dear brother to vomit; it was his obsession with it."

1 *Eretz Yisrael:* The Land of Israel.

2 *Mashiach:* Messiah, the Anointed One. The coming of the Messiah is marked by the restoration of the House of David, the return of the Jews to Israel, and the coming of world peace and universal justice and harmony.

3 *Galut:* Hebrew for "exile" or "captivity." Originally referring only to those Jews taken into captivity in Babylonia in 586 B.C.E., *galut* came to refer to all Jews living outside the Holy Land after the expulsion of the Jews by Rome in 70 C.E.

4 Mount of Olives: Tradition holds that the Messiah will enter Jerusalem through the Gate of Mercy (Golden Gate) across from the Mount of Olives, bringing about the resurrection of the dead in the Mount of Olives cemetery.

5 Shofar: A ram's horn. The horn is blown on various sacred occasions. The sound of the shofar calls upon the people to repent, and it awakens them to God's sovereignty, justice, and saving power.

@ What does the messianic moment smell like? It smells like something new. What does something new smell like? Nothing. If something is new, it cannot be compared to anything else. It is unique, without precedent, and therefore ineffable. What Reb Menachem Mendel smelled was life as usual: the same old frenzied rush of egos and emotions.

☐ Nothing New

In 1777, Reb Menachem Mendel of Vitebsk established a Hasidic community in Tiberias. Living in *Eretz Yisrael*[1] raised hopes for the coming of the *Mashiach*[2] and the redemption of the Jewish people from the *galut*.[3]

After some months, a prankster secretly climbed up the Mount of Olives[4] and blew a great blast from his shofar,[5] signaling that the Messiah had indeed arrived. Word quickly spread through the land, and with it a feverish anticipation. People stopped working, and family matters went unattended. Everyone was obsessed with the news of the Messiah's coming.

When word of the Messiah's arrival reached Tiberias, Reb Menachem Mendel's Hasidim heard it and raced to share the news with their rebbe.

"Rebbe! The shofar was sounded on the Mount of Olives! *Mashiach* is here!"

Expecting their teacher to leap with joy, his Hasidim were surprised to see the rebbe rise slowly from his study table and walk to the window. Throwing open the wooden shutters, Reb Menachem Mendel stuck his head out the window and took in a long, deep breath through his nose as if he were savoring the aroma of a freshly baked pie. He then pulled his head inside and closed the shutters.

Turning to his Hasidim, he said: "My friends, I wish it were true, but I am afraid the *Mashiach* is not yet among us, for I smelled nothing new in the air."

1 *Maggid* (literally, "narrator"): A Hebrew word used for preacher. The Hasidic preachers used dramatic touches and a singsong style of delivery to move their listeners to redouble their efforts for justice and compassion.

2 Shul (literally, "school"): A Yiddish term used by Jews of European descent to refer to any traditional synagogue. Because of the strong educational component of the early synagogue, the Gentiles in the Roman world called the Jewish house of prayer a *schola*.

3 *Shabbos:* The Sabbath.

4 Psalm 16:8: Called the *Shiviti,* this text is often hung in synagogues on a wall in front of the worshippers. It was also used as focal point for meditation, as an amulet, and as a meditative chant: *Shiviti Adonai l'negdi tamid.*

℮ "I am ever mindful of God's Presence." This single line from the Psalms speaks to the heart of Jewish spiritual practice. Among the Hasidim, many repeated this line of the Psalms over and over as a means of seeing through the seemingly diverse nature of reality to the singular core that is God.

Living with the awareness of God's Presence is living the spiritually awakened life. It means seeing the One as the many. It is stepping beyond duality without rejecting duality. It is seeing the nonduality that is God manifest as the duality that is creation. There is nothing other than God. The *Shiviti* rejects nothing: spirit and matter, heaven and earth, the sacred and the secular, the holy and the mundane are all seen as facets of the Divine.

☐ The Sermon

Each year, Reb Yisrael, the *Maqqid*[1] of Koznitz, would visit the town of Apta. On one such visit, the elders of the town asked the rebbe to preach in their shul[2] on *Shabbos*.[3] Reb Yisrael refused, saying: "Last year when I visited you, the same request was made. I spoke in your shul and accomplished nothing. Things are the same today as then; why should I waste my breath?"

Word of the rebbe's harsh rebuke spread swiftly through the town. All of Apta fell into depression. Then a craftsman asked to meet with the *Maggid*.

"I am neither scholar nor saint," the man said to the *Maggid*, "but I can say to you that you are mistaken about your sermon having no effect. I listened to what you said last year. You spoke of the obligation of every Jew to practice what is written in the Psalms: 'I am ever mindful of God's Presence.'[4] From that moment on, I have sought to do just that. The Name of God is constantly before me, revealed as black fire written on white fire in everyone I meet and everything I encounter. I tremble in awe of God's Presence constantly."

The *Maggid* smiled at the man and apologized for his hasty rebuke. "If one heart was opened last year, perhaps two will open this year." The *Maggid* preached at the synagogue that *Shabbos*, and the lives of many were turned toward godliness.

[1] *Perek Shirah:* A tenth-century kabbalistic text that speaks of the earth as a vessel of song that has traveled through space since creation, singing praises of the Creator.

[2] Mitzvah: Divine command.

[3] Proverbs 25:21.

[e] What is your song? And for whom are you willing to die?

No one can answer these questions for you. No one can give you your song, for no one knows it but you. What you can do is invite your song to reveal itself to you by immersing yourself in the songs of others. How can you do this? By listening attentively to life around you.

What of the second question? The frog's death was not a messianic atonement but a personal fulfillment. Feeding his enemy, not dying for his enemy, is the point. Your enemy is the nagging sense of meaninglessness that drives you to quest after power and control. When you sing your song, you find your purpose and meaning in life. All hungers vanish, and you are full and fulfilled.

☐ The Frog's Song

When Dov Ber, the *Maggid* of Mezritch, died, his senior students gathered to share their memories of their teacher. Hours passed, and eventually they fell silent, having exhausted all they could remember.

After a few minutes of silence, Reb Shneur Zalman of Liadi spoke: "Our teacher was a sage of infinite wisdom, but some of his actions can be a bit confusing. For example, we all know that our rebbe used to leave his home at dawn each morning and walk along the lake where the frogs congregate and croak. What I wonder is, do any of you know why he did this?"

The Hasidim looked one to the other, but none spoke.

Reb Shneur Zalman then answered his own question, saying, "This is what I think. We learn from *Perek Shirah*[1] that when King David finished writing the Book of Psalms he called to God and said, 'Is there any creature who sings more praises to You than I?' Suddenly a frog hopped up in front of him and said, 'What arrogance, even for a king! I for one recite far more songs of praise than you, and each of my songs contains three thousand interpretations! And that is not all. My very life fulfills a mitzvah,[2] for there is a creature that lives on the edge of this pond whose very life depends on eating me. When he is hungry I give myself to him in fulfillment of the verse 'If your enemy is hungry, feed him.'[3]

"Every aspect of creation, from the smallest to the greatest, from the inanimate to the animate, carries a melody into this world and sings it each in its own way. Even frogs have their own song."

He paused to see whether his friends were following him. "Don't you see," he said to them, "this was the reason our rebbe walked to the lake each morning? He went to learn the song of the frog, that he might pray among them."

1   *Shulchan Aruch* (literally, "set table"): The standard code of Jewish law *(halachah)* written by Joseph Karo of Safed in the mid-sixteenth century.

2   *Moshe Rabbeinu:* Moses, our Teacher.

☐ Come with Me

Reb Mottel of Kalshin was a successful entrepreneur, who spoke fluent Polish and had connections with powerful ministers in the Polish government. It once happened that the Polish authorities in Warsaw planned to pass a law forcing the Jews to burn all sections of the *Shulchan Aruch*[1] that dealt with civil and criminal law, forcing the Jews to settle matters in Polish courts and thus weakening the authority of their rabbis.

When word of this law reached the Jews, Reb Mottel was summoned to the study of Reb Yitzchak of Vorki. Reb Yitzchak asked him to meet with a certain powerful government official and to convince him to withdraw the bill before it became law.

Terrified, Reb Mottel protested: "Do you know what you are asking? This official is a madman, and his hatred of Jews knows no end. I have heard from others that he vows to kill anyone who goes to him with a request to alter his position on any legislation! To go to him with this is certain death for me, and he will not change his mind."

Reb Yitzchak listened carefully and said, "When *Moshe Rabbeinu*[2] went to Pharaoh to demand that he free his Hebrew slaves, do you think he was unafraid?"

"No," Reb Mottel said. "I am certain that he was afraid. Who would not be?"

(continued on page 53)

51

3 Exodus 9:1.

℮ Where does fear originate? There are some who claim we fear the unknown, but this is impossible. If something is truly unknown, how can we know to fear it? What we really fear is our projection of the known onto the future. We conjure up the worst fears of the past, impose them on the next moment, and respond to them accordingly. In so doing, however, we are responding not to what is, but to what we imagine.

God invites you to imagine differently. Whenever you confront an enemy, God calls to you, saying, "Come to Pharaoh." One who says "come" invites you to be with that one. When God says, "Come to Pharaoh," God is saying, "Come to Me through Pharaoh. Come to Me by engaging the enemy and seeing into the heart of the stranger, that you might find the same heart beating in you both."

God commands us to "know the heart of a stranger" (Exodus 23:9) and to feel solidarity with the stranger, for you, too, know what it is to be a stranger. To know the stranger is to know the enemy. To know the enemy is to know your own heart. To know your own heart is to know that God is both self and stranger, friend and foe.

This knowing fills you with a deep and abiding courage and joy, and it is this joy that embraces the stranger and invites her or him to come to God through you.

"Exactly," the rebbe said. "He was afraid Pharaoh would kill him and nothing good would come of his meeting. It is for this reason that God said to Moshe 'Come to Pharaoh.'3 'Come,' not 'go.' God knew that Moshe was afraid, so God said 'Come *with Me* to Pharaoh,' reminding Moshe that God is always with him. It will be the same with you. If you go to him alone you are doomed, but if you come with God you will succeed."

Reb Mottel's fear melted, and he traveled to Warsaw unafraid. Indeed, so fearless and joyous was he during his meeting with the minister that the official could not summon even an ounce of anger, and he granted Reb Mottel's request on the spot.

1 *Teshuvah* (literally, "turn"): The Hebrew word for repentance. There are two kinds of repentance. Repentance motivated by fear of punishment lessens the severity of the punishment; repentance motivated by love of God transforms sins into merits, for the sins were catalysts to repentance. Thus the sages taught, "The place occupied by one who sins and returns out of love cannot be attained even by the saint who has never sinned at all" (*Berachot* 34b).

2 Exodus 14:15.

@ There are two types of faith: self-powered and other-powered. The first means that salvation (redemption, liberation, realization, etc.) is up to you. The second means that salvation is a gift of grace, and there is nothing you can do to earn it or bring it about.

Which is true? Reb Shlomo Leib sides with the former; Menachem Mendel sides with the latter. Reb Yaakov David just smiles. As chief justice he is skilled at seeing both sides of a case, and in this case both sides are true. Ultimately, awakening is a gift, but it is one for which you must prepare. This preparation is called *teshuvah*, "turning." You must choose to turn from evil and do good (Psalm 34:14). The turning is in your power and your power alone. But the results of this turning are not yours to control. This is where the other-power comes in. You choose to change, and then God gifts you with change.

☐ Why Cry to Me?

Reb Yaakov David, the chief justice of the rabbinic court of Koznitz and a senior student of Reb Shlomo Leib of Linchna, once visited Reb Menachem Mendel of Kotsk. After some time, their conversation turned to Reb Shlomo.

"I am a great admirer of your teacher," the Kotsker Rebbe said, "but there is one thing about him that I do not understand."

Reb Yaakov David said, "I do not pretend to be my teacher's equal, but perhaps I can explain that which confuses you. Please, share it with me."

"Excellent," Menachem Mendel said. "Reb Shlomo is forever calling out to God, asking God to send the Messiah. This is true?"

"Yes, this is very true. My rebbe's passion for messianic redemption is greater than all of ours put together."

"Good. So here is my dilemma: If the rebbe is so concerned with messianic redemption, why does he entreat God? Better to call to the Jews and urge them toward *teshuvah*.[1] After all, when *Moshe Rabbeinu* called out to God at the shore of the Red Sea, God said to him: 'Why do you cry out to Me? Speak to the Children of Israel...!'"[2]

Reb Yaakov David smiled and said nothing.

1 Exodus 14:30.

2 Exodus 14:31.

🌀 There are two kinds of spirituality. One rests on the certainty of God's saving grace. The other rests on nothing at all. The woman in this story represents the first; Reb Shalom represents the second. In Hebrew, these two types of faith care called *emunah* and *bittachon*.

Emunah is faith in something. *Bittachon* is simply, and literally, trust. For one to have *emunah*, there must be a "something" in which one believes. *Bittachon* relies on nothing other than the belief that whatever happens to us is, in and of itself, the way to salvation if we would but engage it with our full attention.

Bittachon is a very difficult state to attain. Reb Shalom was asking something of this woman that even the Israelites could not give. Even though they had just witnessed the power of God displayed through the Ten Plagues, the Israelites could not trust God and engage the challenge of the moment head on. Instead, they panicked and asked God to save them once again.

Asking God for help is a sign of faith, just not the deepest faith. Reb Shalom had forgotten how hard *bittachon* is to achieve. The woman reminded him that most people need more than trust; we need signs. Given her situation, *emunah* was enough. Given your situation, which would you prefer?

☐ Show Me

A woman once visited Reb Shalom of Belz on an urgent matter of personal concern.

"I have done all I can do in this matter, Rebbe," she said, "If I am to succeed and survive, it will be only because of God's aid, and I can only get that with your aid. Please, Rebbe, pray to God on my behalf!"

The rebbe refused, saying, "The essential thing, good woman, is to have faith."

The woman was shocked. She was a good and decent person, and one in true need. There could be no good reason for the rebbe to turn down her plea for help.

Taking a deep breath, the woman said, "Far be it from me to argue with my rebbe..."

"But you will do so anyway?" Reb Shalom barked. "Do you think you know this situation better than me?"

"I am not a learned woman," she replied evenly, "but I do know a bit of Torah. When our ancestors were about to be slaughtered by Pharaoh's army at the shores of the Red Sea, Torah first says that God 'saved' them[1] and only later says that they believed in God.[2] Their salvation preceded their faith. I am no different. If God would save me now in this situation, I will without doubt have faith as well."

"What is this?" Reb Shalom yelled. "An illiterate woman seeks to teach me Torah? No one has ever bested me in Torah study!" The woman stood and waited, neither arguing her point nor turning to leave. Suddenly the rebbe's face broke into a great smile. He laughed loudly and said, "No one, that is, until now! No one, that is, but you!"

The rebbe prayed for the woman's welfare, and God granted all she needed.

1 *Beis midrash:* Communal house of study.

2 Talmud: The authoritative collection of Jewish law and lore compiled around the year 500 C.E. and containing teachings spanning the previous seven hundred years. The word *Talmud* comes from the Hebrew root *l-m-d,* meaning to study or to teach.

3 *Misnaged* (literally, "opponent;" plural *misnagedim*): A derogatory term applied by the Hasidim to their traditionalist adversaries in Eastern Europe. The *misnagedim* opposed the "cult" of the rebbe, the introduction of rites common to Oriental (Sephardi) Jews, and the lack of emphasis on scholarship.

4/5 Exodus 15:2.

@ The spiritual journey begins with a radical call to freedom: "God said to Abram, 'Go from your country, from your kin, from your father's house to the land that I will show you'" (Genesis 12:1). If Abram was to follow God, he must free himself from everything that made him who he was: the norms of his country, tribe, and family.

God is the unconditioned and unconditionable. God is whatever God will be (Exodus 3:14) and cannot be fixed into any system of thought. So, too, the divine spark is within you. You are the image and likeness of God; you, too, are essentially and radically free, and only when you realize that freedom do you realize your potential as God manifest. You honor your past by claiming your destiny, not by imitating the old but by embracing the new and uncharted.

☐ The Hidden Spark

During a visit with Reb Yaakov Yitzchak, the *Chozeh* of Lublin, a school-master from Goray, was told, "There exists in your town a hidden spark of God that needs nurturing. Locate this spark and bring it to me."

Understanding Reb Yaakov Yitzchak to mean that Goray was home to a fledgling saint, the schoolmaster returned home and spent the night hiding in the *beis midrash*.[1] "If there is a hidden saint among us," he thought to himself, "he will surely come to study when all others have gone home to sleep."

That night Menachem Mendel, an odd fellow thought to be illiterate and perhaps insane, entered the *beis midrash*. Opening a volume of Talmud,[2] he stood on one foot and entered into pure ecstasy as he read aloud from the text. The schoolmaster was stunned. To be certain this was not a fluke, he spent several nights in hiding; each night at midnight Menachem Mendel sneaked into the *beis midrash* and slipped into paradise.

On the fourth night, a bit of dust lodged in the schoolmaster's throat, and he coughed aloud. Menachem Mendel slammed his book closed, leaped over to the stove, and began clapping his hands loudly and babbling insanely. The schoolmaster came out of hiding and spoke to him: "Please stop. I am not here to reveal your secret but to tell you that the *Chozeh* of Lublin wishes me to take you to him." Menachem Mendel set out immediately for Lublin.

When Menachem Mendel's father, a *misnaged*,[3] heard of his son's departure, he rode off after him hoping to bring him back home. Finding his son, he said, "Why are you forsaking the tradition of your fathers?"

Menachem Mendel replied softly and firmly, "I am following the teaching of Torah. First, Torah tells us 'This is my God and I will praise Him.'[4] Only later do we read 'This is my father's God, and I will exalt Him.'"[5]

1 Dov Ber of Mezritch (1704 [?]–1772): Known as the *Maggid* (Preacher) of Mezritch, Dov Ber succeeded the Baal Shem Tov after the latter's death and created the institution of rebbe, charismatic leaders of independent Hasidic communities.

2 Nothing: The Hebrew word for nothing, *ayn,* is also one of the kabbalistic names of God, *Ayn,* the No-thing that gives rise to all things. Reb Aharon is not simply making a claim for deep humility; he is also identifying with the One Who is the many.

@ Who are you? This question is at the heart of the spiritual quest, and your answer to it determines the quality of your life. Reb Aharon learned who he was from the *Maggid* of Mezritch. "I am nothing." But there is more to this than simple nihilism.

In Hebrew the word for "I" is *ani.* The word for "nothing" is *ayn.* *Ayn* is also one of the kabbalistic Names of God, as in *Ayn Sof,* the No-thing Without End. God is the No-thing that is all things. The kabbalists noticed that *ani* and *ayn* are both composed of the same three Hebrew letters: *aleph, nun,* and *yud.* When different words share the same letters, they are thought to share a deep unity. The only difference between *ani* and *ayn,* self and nothing, is the order of the letters. When the *yud* is at the end of the word, there is "I." When the *yud* is in the middle of the word, there is "nothing."

The *yud* stands for *yadah,* consciousness. When consciousness is focused outward, "I" emerges. When consciousness is focused inward, "God" is present. So who are you: the outer I or the inner Nothing? The answer is that you are both. The challenge is to see the Nothing in the other when you are *ani*; and the self in the Nothing when you are *Ayn.*

☐ Nothing

Reb Aharon of Karlin visited his rebbe, the *Maggid* of Mezritch,[1] as often as he could. Returning home from one such visit, Reb Aharon was besieged by a great crowd of friends and fellow Hasidim.

"Tell us what you have learned, Reb Aharon!" they cried. "Tell us what you have learned!"

When the crowd grew quiet, that all might hear what Reb Aharon would impart to them, he said, "I learned nothing."

Not sure they understood him, his friends asked again, "What did you learn from the *Maggid*?"

Again Reb Aharon waited for silence. And again he said, "Nothing."

Certain that Reb Aharon was denying them some great teaching, his friends said sarcastically, "So you bother to make these many trips to Mezritch so that you can learn nothing?"

"Exactly," Reb Aharon replied. "I gained the knowledge that I am nothing."[2]

1 Sava Kaddisha of Radoshitz (1765–1843): The Holy Grandfather, or the Holy Old Man, Sava Kaddisha was a miracle worker who lived in poverty.

2 *Ruach HaKodesh:* The Holy Spirit. The Hebrew Bible makes more than eighty references to the Holy Spirit (or *Ruach Elohim, Ruach Adonai,* the Spirit of God), a power that manifests in individuals and allows them to carry out a divine command. The Rabbis said that with the last of the Prophets (Haggai, Zechariah, and Malachi), *Ruach HaKodesh* would manifest in the *tzaddikim,* the righteous of each generation: "Piety leads to the Holy Spirit" (*Mishnah Sota* 9:15), and "All that the *tzaddikim* do, they do with the power of the Holy Spirit" (*Tanhuma, Va-Yehi* 13). The power of the *Ruach HaKodesh* allows one to see into the future, to bestow blessings on the needy, and to discern the spiritual source of creation.

@ What makes a rebbe a rebbe? What makes a rebbe a rebbe is the willingness and ability to stand without pretense before yourself and before God.

Our sense of self is so distorted by the illusion of being separate from God that we take anyone who demonstrates even a modicum of wisdom for a saint, and we mistake hubris for spiritual superiority. There is no less or more in God. We are all equally of the One. Where we differ is in our awareness of this truth. But the more aware we are of our innate divinity, the less we are raised up above others. To see the self as God is to know the other as God as well. A true rebbe is one who can read not only the hearts and minds of his Hasidim but his own heart and mind as well. It is in not knowing the latter that the real danger lies.

☐ The New Rebbe

When the Sava Kaddisah of Radoshitz[1] died, his son Reb Yisrael Yitzchak succeeded him as rebbe. Two Hasidim set out by carriage to visit the new rebbe, just as they had done many times before during the lifetime of the old rebbe. As they drew closer to Radoshitz, they began to have doubts about this new rebbe.

"It is not that I doubt the judgment of the Old Rebbe," the one said to his friend, "and I respect his choice of his son to succeed him; it is just that he was so steeped in *Ruach HaKodesh*[2] that I wonder whether his son can truly lead us in the same manner."

"You are not the only one with doubts," the other said. "The Old Man could read minds. When I went to see him for advice, he listened not only to the words of my mouth but also to the thoughts in my brain."

"And not just that," the first Hasid said, "but the hidden thoughts of the heart as well. We were transparent to the Old Rebbe, and is it right for us to expect the same from his son?"

Their doubts grew, but as they had already ridden most of the way to Radoshitz, they decided it was wiser to continue than to return home. After all, the rebbe was the son of their beloved teacher, and to spend one *Shabbos* with him was only proper.

As they entered the rebbe's house, Reb Yisrael Yitzchak greeted them, saying, "So what if my father could read the thoughts of those who traveled to see him? Is that enough to make him worthy of being a rebbe? Are you so hungry for signs that you are willing to settle for magicians' tricks?"

1 | *Melamed:* Tutor.

2 | Exodus 18:12.

3 | Psalm 72:19.

4 | *Tzaddik* (from *tzedek*, justice): A saint. Hasidism considered their rebbes to be *tzaddikim* (plural of *tzaddik*).

@ | The whole world is filled with Divine Presence—not that life contains God, but that God contains all life. God suffuses life the way wet suffuses water. God is the very essence of reality. Because of this suffusion, we often are unaware of God in, with, and as all things.

We may be unaware of God in the same way a bird may be unaware of the air or a fish unaware of the sea. That is why we are willing to go through such stringent spiritual disciplines: We have to do something strange in order to finally see that which is common. Yet, we sometimes become so infatuated with the discipline that we forget it is a means to something else. This is when spirituality and religion become idolatrous; the sign replaces the thing toward which it points.

In Hasidism, the rebbe is a gateway to God. Levi Yitzchak's invitation to Reb Baruch was an invitation to move closer to God. Reb Baruch feared, and Reb Elimelech confirmed, that it is all too easy to get attached to the gateway and forget to walk through it.

☐ Eating in the Presence of God

Reb Baruch, the *Maggid* of Rika, was the *melamed*[1] to the household of Reb Levi Yitzchak of Berditchev. When his contract with the rebbe was to be renewed, the rebbe added a stipulation that Reb Baruch would eat with him from the same plate—a great honor. Reb Baruch asked for some time to consider the matter.

At just this time, Berditchev was host to two other famous sages, Reb Elimelech of Lyzhansk and his brother, Reb Zusya of Hanipoli. Reb Baruch decided to ask their advice regarding his eating with the rebbe.

As he approached the attic room where they were staying, he heard Reb Elimelech say to his brother, "Torah teaches: 'Aharon and all the elders of Israel came to eat bread with the father-in-law of Moshe in the Presence of God.'[2] The Talmudic sages ask why Torah says 'in the Presence of God' when it should have said 'in the presence of Moshe.' They answer their own question, saying that Torah is teaching us that whenever one eats with sages he eats in the Presence of God.

"Now, brother," Reb Elimelech continued, "I have a problem with their understanding. How could the Talmud doubt that they ate in God's Presence? The whole universe is filled with God;[3] wherever one eats, one eats in the Divine Presence. To my mind, what the Talmud is really asking is whether Aharon and the elders knew they were eating in the Presence of God, or whether they were distracted from this by eating in the presence of Moshe."

Hearing this, Reb Baruch suddenly knew the answer to his own question. He returned to the rebbe and respectfully declined his offer. "Sometimes," he said, "it is not wise to eat in the presence of a *tzaddik*."[4]

@ How do you handle the mud in your life?

Reb Meir says it is best to look sharp and avoid the mud in the first place. Reb Yisrael says it is better to prepare for the mud in advance and just force your way through. Both are right, and even taken together, neither is complete.

Reb Meir teaches us that not every muddy road need be traveled. If we are diligent and thoughtful, we can see the mud before we fall into it and take the trouble to detour around it. This is especially good advice when it comes to speech. If we stop and consider the impact of our words before uttering those words, we will avoid some very sticky situations.

Reb Yisrael reminds us that no matter how careful we are, there will be times when we get stuck in the mud. At these times, it pays to have the strength to pull yourself free. This is especially true when it comes to matters of finances. If we take care to put aside money when we have it to help us when we don't, we will avoid some very uncomfortable times ahead.

Good advice from both our rebbes. Yet, no matter how vigilant we are, no matter how strong and prepared we become, there are times when the mud will overwhelm us. In these cases, you will just have to get into the mud with your horse and pull.

☐ Avoiding the Mud

Reb Meir of Premishlan and Reb Yisrael of Ruzhin were the best of friends, yet no two people could be more different. Reb Meir lived in great poverty. He never allowed even a penny to spend the night in his house but would rush outside to give it to the poor. Reb Yisrael, on the other hand, lived like a king.

These two friends once met as each was preparing to take a journey. Reb Meir was sitting on a simple cart drawn by one scrawny horse. Reb Yisrael was housed in a rich lacquered coach pulled by four powerful stallions.

Reb Yisrael walked over to the horse hitched to Reb Meir's wagon. With mock concern, he inspected the horse with great care. Then he turned to his friend and with barely concealed humor said to him, "I always travel with four strong horses. In this way, if my coach should become stuck in the mud they will be able to free it quickly. I can see, however, that your horse seems barely able to carry you and your wagon on a dry and hard-packed road. There is bound to be mud on your travels. Why do you take such risks?"

Reb Meir stepped down from his wagon and walked over to his friend, who was still standing next to Reb Meir's horse. Placing his arms around his beloved old horse's neck, Reb Meir said softly, "The risk, I think, is yours. Because I travel with this one horse that in no way can free this wagon if it becomes stuck in the mud, I am very careful to avoid the mud in the first place. You, my friend, are certain you can get free if stuck and thus do not look where you are going."

1 *Alef-beis:* The Hebrew alphabet.

@ Reb Menachem Mendel's grandson finds himself in the classic double bind that is key to all spiritual awakening. He knows that only by surrendering the "I," the self, can he experience God; and he knows that as long as it is the self that is doing the surrendering, no real surrender is possible. If the self is first, if "I" initiates everything, including surrender, then there is no escape from ego and no hope of experiencing God.

Yet, Torah opens with a very different picture of reality. The first words of Genesis are *Bereshit bara Elohim,* "In the beginning God created..." Here, God is clearly first. So who is right: the rebbe's grandson or the Torah? There seems to be something true about both positions, yet they seem to be mutually exclusive. And that is the bind. The way out is to accept them both, which is what Torah does in a later passage: *Anochi Adonai Elohecha,* "I am the Lord your God" (Exodus 20:2).

Anochi, itself, is God! When you realize that God is all in all, then the true nature of the "I" is revealed, and the selfishness that arises from thinking you are other than God is no more. God and self are not mutually exclusive; self is simply one of the ways God is present in the world.

☐ The Alphabet of Sorrow

It once happened that one of the grandsons of Reb Menachem Mendel of Lubavitch fell into a deep funk. His friends came to lift his spirits.

"What can it be that is causing you this great sadness?" they asked.

"The *alef-beis*,"[1] he replied.

"The alphabet?" they exclaimed. "We all learned the *alef-beis* when we were children, and we are not depressed because of it. What do you know that we do not?"

"Not the whole alphabet," the young Hasid said, "just the first two letters, *alef* and *beis*."

Seeing that his friends had no idea what he was talking about, he continued: "The *alef* stands for *Anochi*, 'I'; the *beis* stands for *bereshit*, 'in the beginning.' Now do you see why I am so upset?"

His friends looked one to the other to see whether anyone had even the slightest inkling of what their friend was talking about. They finally returned their eyes to him and shrugged.

"This is what troubles me," the boy said. "The 'I' is always 'in the beginning' of everything we do. Every beginning, every venture, is preceded by the ego and selfishness. How am I ever to act selflessly when all efforts are tainted from the beginning?"

1 Besht: An acronym for Baal Shem Tov.

2 *Mitzvos*: Divine commandments.

3 *Derekh eretz* (literally, "the way of the world"): Deeds that are intrinsically good, though not commanded by God (those being *mitzvos*). Among the deeds the Rabbis highlighted as *derekh eretz* are courtesy (*Berachot* 6b), personal hygiene (*Avodah Zara* 20b), respect for women (*Shabbat* 10b), honoring parents and teachers (*Sanhedrin* 100b), avoiding coarse speech (*Pesach* 3a), and good manners (*Yoma* 4b).

℮ The Hasidim teach that the soul manifests in the world through Three Garments: thought, word, and deed. When the soul is healthy, your thoughts are positive, your words are compassionate, and your deeds are just. When the soul is weak, the Garments become soiled: thoughts become obsessive; words become hurtful; and deeds become arrogant, greedy, and mean. How is the soul weakened? When you willfully think, speak, and act contrary to the natural inclination of a healthy soul, you cause the soul to weaken. As the soul weakens, sinful thoughts, words, and deeds become more and more natural, more and more an expression of a diseased soul.

Healing comes when the soul is made right and returned to its pure state. How? The Baal Shem Tov had the ability to intervene and do this directly. But you cannot rely on finding someone of his caliber to heal you. You can heal yourself by cleansing the Garments of the Soul and rectifying the soul itself: think positively, speak kindly, and act graciously. In time, your soul will return to its pure state and empower you to turn from evil and do good (Psalm 34:14).

☐ A Healing Broth

The Baal Shem Tov was passing through a town in which a man lay critically ill. Word of the Besht's[1] arrival spread quickly, and the man's doctor asked the Baal Shem Tov to visit his patient.

The Baal Shem Tov came to see the man and looked at him for a brief moment. He then turned to the man's wife and asked her to prepare some chicken broth for her husband. The man sipped some of the soup and immediately began to speak. The Baal Shem Tov stayed with him for a few hours, during which the man's health returned.

As the Baal Shem Tov prepared to leave, the man's doctor asked for a moment of his time. "I know this man was close to death," the doctor said. "There was nothing I could do, and certainly chicken soup would not be enough to cure him. What did you do?"

The Baal Shem Tov said: "Illness appears in the body but is caused by the spirit. You looked at the man as a body; I looked at him as a soul. When a man uses his body in ungodly ways—acting without thinking, speaking cruelly, violating the mitzvos[2] and derekh eretz[3]—then his spirit suffers and cannot keep the body well. This was the case with your patient. I spoke to his soul and urged it to turn from selfishness to selflessness. As soon as it agreed, the body responded by returning to health."

"And the soup?" the doctor asked.

The Baal Shem Tov simply smiled, shrugged, and took his leave.

1 *Cholent* (from the French word for "hot"): A thick stew that could be prepared on Friday and left simmering all day Saturday, developed by the Jews of southern France in response to the law prohibiting lighting a fire on the Sabbath.

2 Challah: Twisted loaf of bread prepared especially for the Sabbath.

☐ A Holy Appetite

It once happened that Reb Avigdor Halberstam, the brother of Reb Chaim of Zanz, was invited to spend *Shabbos* at the home of a man known for his wealth but not his compassion. He was infamous for treating his servants harshly and firing them for the slightest mistake.

As was the custom in those days, the cook prepared a *cholent*[1] for *Shabbos* lunch. In deference to their guest, the cook passed the pot of stew to Reb Avigdor, who was expected to ladle it out to the host, the family, and any other guests present.

The rebbe breathed deeply of its aroma. Instead of ladling the stew, however, he took a spoon and tasted some right from the pot. "How unusual!" he cried and ate some more. "This is the best *cholent* I have ever tasted!" And as his host and Hasidim watched in amazement, he ate all the *cholent* in the pot, leaving nothing for the rest of them.

Rather than apologize, Reb Avigdor turned to the cook and said, "Fabulous! Perhaps you have a bit more?" The woman brought out the last of the *cholent*, and the rabbi ate it all.

The host and his family were stunned. Never had they had a guest behave this way, and certainly not one of Reb Avigdor's stature. Yet, in deference to their guest, they said nothing and made do with challah.[2]

(continued on page 75)

73

| 3 | *Chazzir:* A pig.

| @ | How important is your reputation? Are you willing to look the fool to protect another from undeserved retribution? Are you sure?

There are many stories of rebbes, saints, gurus, and the like acting crazy in order to make a point. So many, in fact, that we have a term for this: crazy wisdom. The craziness of crazy wisdom refers to its flying in the face of convention. The problem with crazy wisdom is how to tell whether the wisdom is crazy or the sage is simply insane.

Reb Avigdor's Hasidim were willing to give him the benefit of the doubt during dinner, but afterward they demanded to know what was going on. This is a good model for all of us.

Reb Avigdor's willingness to play the *chazzir* to protect another from unjust punishment shows that he was bigger than his reputation. He would take the bad press and know that his motives were just. Moreover, he was willing to explain himself to his students. He could have said, "Never question my judgment!" Instead, he honored their need to know and explained the reasons for his crazy behavior. This is a way to test all our spiritual teachers: Are they willing to explain themselves to us, and are their explanations rooted in justice and compassion?

After *Shabbos,* the rabbi and his students thanked the family for their hospitality and left. When they were outside the town, the Hasidim asked the rebbe about his bizarre behavior. "When our host passed me the pot of *cholent,*" the rebbe said, "its aroma smelled of kerosene. It was clear to me that the cook had mistakenly added this to our food rather than vinegar. If I allowed our host to taste the *cholent* he would have fired the girl on the spot. So I ate the whole thing to save her job. They can think of me whatever they wish, but of this young girl they should imagine that her skills are so fine as to cause a rabbi to act like a *chazzir.*"[3]

1 *Misnaged:* An opponent of Hasidism.

2 *Kohen HaGadol:* High Priest. The first High Priest was Aaron (Exodus 28:1), and all subsequent High Priests were required to be descendents of Aaron. After the fall of the Temple (70 c.e.), the Rabbis taught that the sanctity of the sacrificial altar shifted to the dinner table. Preparing and eating meals with the required prayers before and after eating, and focusing table talk on words of Torah, elevated eating to a spiritual discipline equivalent to that of a High Priest serving in the Temple.

☐ Seeing or Believing

Reb Meir was a Hasid of Reb Mordechai of Lechovitch. He was also the occasional business partner of Reb Gershon, who was a devout *misnaged*.[1]

Reb Meir was always inviting his partner to join him on his many visits to his rebbe, but Reb Gershon's hatred of Hasidism was so strong that he could never consent to visiting his partner's rebbe. Not wishing to hurt the feelings of his friend, he would find many reasons to explain why travel to Lechovitch was out of the question.

It once happened, however, that separate business matters brought both men to Lechovitch on the same day. Discovering that his friend would be in town at the same time as himself, Reb Meir once again invited Reb Gershon to visit his rebbe. Seeing no way out that would not be offensive to Reb Meir, Reb Gershom agreed.

When the two men arrived at Reb Mordechai's house, they were ushered into the rebbe's dining room, where he was just beginning to eat his dinner. Reb Meir urged his partner to speak to the rebbe, to ask a question, to say something, but Reb Gershon was clearly in a state of pure ecstasy. After a few minutes they left the rebbe's house.

Reb Meir said to his friend: "What happened to you in there?"

Reb Gershon said, "I saw the rebbe eating with the holiness of the *Kohen HaGadol!*"[2]

(continued on page 79)

| ℮ | What did Reb Gershon see? He saw Reb Mordechai eating with an awareness of God's Presence equal to that of the *Kohen HaGadol,* the High Priest of ancient Israel. What did Reb Meir see? He saw the same thing but did not recognize it as anything out of the ordinary. It is not that Reb Meir didn't see what Reb Gershon saw, but, unlike Reb Gershon, he saw nothing unusual about it. When his partner was so moved by what was for him an everyday event, Reb Meir began to doubt the quality of his own seeing. His rebbe then shifted Reb Meir's attention from seeing to trusting.

Trust is about the unknown; seeing is about the known. If you see a bus coming down the street, you do not say, "I trust the bus is coming." You say, "Look, here comes the bus." It makes no sense to trust what you know. Trust matters only in relation to what you don't know. And that is what makes it a higher spiritual quality than sight, but also a more dangerous one.

Albert Einstein said there is one fundamental question we must ask of the universe: Is it friendly or not? We cannot answer that question once and for all. All we can do is take life as an experiment. All good experiments begin with a hypothesis. In this case, the hypothesis is that the universe is friendly, that it is conducive to human life, love, and meaning. To test this hypothesis, you have to live as if it were so and see what happens. You have to trust that your hypothesis is true, and then risk the consequences of its being false. This is what makes spiritual life so dangerous. It is life on the edge of trust.

Shocked, Reb Meir turned from his partner and ran back to the rebbe. When he arrived he said, "Rebbe, here I come to see you as often as I can, and never have I seen the way you serve the Holy One, Blessed Be He. And yet my *misnaged* partner comes for a minute, under duress, and he sees the miracle of your eating. Is this fair?"

Reb Mordechai said, "It is not about fairness, my friend. Your partner is a *misnaged;* he has to see the truth with his eyes. You, on the other hand, are a Hasid; you have to trust."

1 *Eliyahu haNavi:* Elijah the Prophet.

2 *Kfitzas haderekh:* Shrinking the path. Time and space are not absolutes in the theology of the Baal Shem Tov. They are attributes of God experienced by human beings while God, Itself, embraces and transcends them. The Besht had the capacity to experience the nonduality of God, wherein the seeming duality of "here" and "there," and "now" and "then," are transcended. Thus he could shift time and place as a matter of consciousness. Knowing this would frighten the common folk, he hid his power and traveled by coach. Nevertheless, his horses and close disciples knew that a ride with the Besht was unusual, to say the least.

@ For the Hasid, spiritual pride is the greatest roadblock on the spiritual journey. As we engage in this or that spiritual exercise, we imagine ourselves growing more holy. This is pride. The quality of your spiritual practice rests on the quality of your intention. And there is only one right intention: to do what you do for its own sake, what Judaism calls *lishmah.* To engage in a spiritual practice with the intent of gaining something in return is to practice idolatry.

This is what the fellow in Simcha Bunem's story was doing. He fasted to merit meeting Elijah the Prophet. This is an act of hubris. His egotism made him no smarter than the Baal Shem Tov's horses, who thought it was their strength and not his spirit that moved them.

Now, how does this apply to you? Where do you find yourself spiritually proud? Where do you let it drop that you are a student of this or that, a disciple of one guru or another, or perhaps even a teacher of some esoteric discipline? Where do you worship at the altar of spiritual success and one-upmanship? Wherever it is, recognize it and let it go. Then go get yourself something to eat.

☐ To Be an Angel

Reb Simcha Bunem once spoke to his Hasidim, saying:

"A fellow once came to see me, complaining that even after fasting for forty days he still failed to have a vision of *Eliyahu haNavi*,[1] as promised in the holy books. I said to him, 'Let me tell you a story.'

"The Baal Shem Tov, may his memory be for a blessing, once set out on a long journey. As you know, the Baal Shem Tov had the power of *kfitzas haderekh*,[2] the power to bend space so that he could travel great distances in moments. Yet, he still traveled by horse-drawn carriage in order to disguise his ability.

"On this particular journey, his horses began to speak among themselves. 'Ordinary horses are fed at every village, and yet we pass through them without stopping. Perhaps we are not horses at all but humans who will eat at a fine inn.'

"When they passed by one inn after another, they thought 'Well, perhaps we are not humans but angels, for angels travel as we do and neither eat nor drink.'

"At last they arrived at their destination. The horses were led into the stable, and bags of oats were placed before them. They ate just like famished horses.

"'And so,' I said to this fellow, 'it is the same with you. You fast and imagine yourself an angel worthy of meeting the Prophet Eliyahu. And yet, when you complete your fast, you gulp your food like a horse.'

"Do you understand? Is this man any different from the rest of us?"

1 Mitzvah: Divine commandment.

2 Each morning, observant Jews say, *"Elohai neshamah sh'natatabi t'horah he:* God, the soul You plant within me is pure."* Your soul is pure, transparent to the Divine. Yet, the way the soul is expressed in the world is often tainted with ego. The soul manifests in three ways, called the Three Garments of the Soul: thought, word, and deed. When these are done selflessly, they, like the soul itself, are transparent to God and allow the Light of the Divine to flow through them. Your thoughts are free of selfishness; your words are free of deceit; your actions are free of coercion. But when the Garments are stained by selfishness, dishonesty, and exploitation, the purity of the soul no longer shines through them. The Garments become opaque, and God appears hidden from the world. It is not that the Divine Light no longer shines; it is that you no longer allow the Divine Light to shine through you.

℮ Here is the essence of spiritual life: putting others first and acting *lishmah,* for the sake of the deed and not for the sake of yourself.

The self is like the foam on the crest of a wave: a natural consequence of the nature of the ocean. You would not think to erase the foam any more than you would think to increase the foam. You just accept it as it is for what it is. The same is true of the self. You cannot erase it; you are it. You need not starve it or feed it; just let it be.

Letting the self be is acting *lishmah:* acting with the self but not for the self. Acting *lishmah* does not increase or decrease the self, it simply allows it to function as it was intended: as a vehicle through which God can act godly.

☐ Placing the Self

Reb Yisrael of Ruzhin paid a surprise visit to his Hasidim and found them sitting around a table, idly eating and drinking. The rebbe frowned, clearly disappointed at the actions of his students.

One among them stood and said, "Rebbe, I heard Reb Pinchas of Korets once say that a gathering such as this—Hasidim reveling in friendship—could be likened to the mitzvah[1] of Torah study."

Reb Yisrael said, "I would not think to contradict Reb Pinchas, but the analogy depends on how the thing is done."

"But all we are doing is talking and eating," another student said. "As long as we recite the proper benediction, how can we do this incorrectly?"

Reb Yisrael replied, "It is a matter of intention. If you place yourself last that others may go first, then your act is selfless and holy. If you place yourself first, it is selfish and smacks of idolatry. If you do something for another or for God with no thought of reward or gain, you are hallowing the deed and uplifting the act. In that case, your action is holy. When you do something to further your own ends, you are debasing the deed and concealing the Divine. In that case, your action is sinful."

Still not satisfied, the Hasid said, "Rebbe, what if my action is itself sinful but my intention is pure? What if, heaven forbid, I speak ill of another to save a friend from being hurt. Is that a sin or not?"

"Intention is everything," Reb Yisrael said. "If your intention is for the sake of heaven—that is, if it is for the good of the other and not to benefit yourself—even a sinful act can reveal the Light of God."[2]

1 Torah (from the Hebrew root *yaroh*, "to teach"): Best understood as "teaching" or "instruction." The notion that Torah is primarily a legal code is false and misleading. It is a book of teaching about life and how best to live it, and it contains law but is not limited to law. Technically, Torah refers to the Five Books of Moses, but it is commonly used to refer to the entire body of Jewish teaching.

@ Why did Menachem Mendel find reading Torah with glasses problematic? Wouldn't it make more sense to wear the glasses so that he might see the Word more clearly? His reasoning was this: God created me with weak eyes for a reason. What could this reason be? When I read Torah, my eyesight being what it is, I sometimes misread a word or even an entire sentence. Not knowing I have done this, I then go on to interpret my reading to reveal its deepest truths. Sometimes these revelations are deep insights into the nature of life and how best to live it. They are of enormous benefit to both me and my Hasidim. Now, I would not have seen these truths if, every time I read Torah, I did so in exactly the same way—something that would inevitably happen if I wore glasses. So God gave me weak eyes that I might see things missed by stronger eyes.

Understanding his teacher's reasoning, Reb Eliyahu also read Torah as God intended him to: without glasses and with weak eyes. But outside of study, he wore his glasses so that he might see the world more clearly and meet it more honestly.

How do you read Torah, God's revelation? Do you prefer to see things as others do, sharing the conventional 20/20 worldview of corrected vision? Or are you willing to make mistakes and discover new truths? And if you are willing to do this with the Word, are you willing to do it with the world?

☐ Direct Seeing

As he grew into old age, Reb Menachem Mendel of Kotsk found it more and more difficult to see. He visited an eye doctor in Warsaw, who advised him to wear glasses whenever he studied Torah. In this way, the doctor assured him, he would save what little eyesight he had left.

The Kotsker refused, saying, "Nothing shall come between my eyes and the Torah!"[1]

Reb Eliyahu of Viskit, a disciple of the Kotsker rebbe, had a similar problem with his eyes and visited the same doctor in Warsaw. He was given the same advice. Citing the precedent of his rebbe, Reb Eliyahu, too, refused to wear glasses when he studied Torah. But out of deference to the learned doctor, he chose to wear them at all other times.

1 *Eliyahu haNavi:* Elijah the Prophet. According to the Hebrew Bible, Elijah never died but was taken bodily into heaven. For millennia, Jews have believed that Elijah regularly returns to earth to honor the pious and to teach the ardent seeker.

2 Sabbath Bride, or Queen: Thought to be the embodiment of the *Shekhinah*, the Divine Presence in the world. Among the kabbalists of sixteenth-century Safed, it was customary to go out into the fields on Friday at twilight to welcome the Sabbath Bride. This custom can be traced back over a thousand years to Rabbi Hanina, who would stand at sunset on Friday and say, "Come, let us go forth and welcome the Sabbath Queen," and Rabbi Yannai, who would do the same saying, "Come, Bride! Come, Bride!" (*Shabbat* 119a). Today we honor these Rabbis and their practices with the singing of *Lecha Dodi* (Come Beloved), a mystic hymn written in Safed by Solomon Alkabets (1505–1584).

@ To the Hasidim of Poland, encountering Elijah as a Polish squire was scandalous. Polish squires were infamous for their boorishness and anti-Semitic violence. That, of course, simply makes the Baal Shem Tov's point all the more powerful: Nothing is as it seems; nothing is beyond the reach of God's redemptive power.

What does Elijah say to those he meets? He says what he says. There is no way to communicate it secondhand. Either you see him or you don't. The key is to keep your eyes open. Always.

☐ The Prophetic Squire

The Baal Shem Tov would often converse with the *Eliyahu haNavi* [1] His disciples begged him to share one of these visits with them. After much nagging, he agreed.

One Friday afternoon, as was the custom, the Besht led his students into the fields to greet the Sabbath Bride.[2] As they walked, the Baal Shem Tov said, "I would like to smoke a pipe, but I have forgotten to bring mine with me. Do any of you have a pipe I can borrow?" None did. The Besht then pointed out a Polish squire walking nearby, saying, "Please ask the squire if he has a pipe I can borrow."

It was not the custom of Polish nobles to have much to do with Jews, but this gentleman agreed and followed the students to their teacher that he might give it to him personally. The squire filled the pipe and lit it with the spark of two flints. As he smoked, the Baal Shem Tov asked the squire about the year's harvest and whether the threshing houses were yielding much grain. The Hasidim quickly grew bored and wandered off. When they returned, the squire had departed.

"There," the Besht said, "I have kept my promise. That squire was Eliyahu."

"What?" his students cried. "And you did not tell us?"

"If you had not ignored him you would have known and understood the two questions I asked him. When I inquired after the year's harvest, I was asking whether people have turned their souls toward heaven. When I asked him about the yield of grain, I was asking whether the piety of our prayers was calling down the blessings of divine grace."

"And what did he say?" the Hasidim asked in astonishment.

"He said what he said," the Besht said.

1 *Ribbono shel Olam:* Master of the Universe (God).

2 Malachi 3:7; Zechariah 1:3.

3 Siddur: Hebrew prayer book.

@ The feeling of being in exile from God is part of the human condition, but it is only a feeling, a perception—and a misperception at that. It arises from our misunderstanding of the nature of God and creation. We imagine that God is separate from creation in the way a potter is separate from her pots. But God is infinite and without boundaries, and hence incapable of being separate from, or other than, anything. God is everything; yet, given God's infinite creativity, everything that God is is unique. Just as no two waves are exactly alike and yet all waves are a manifestation of the ocean, so, too, no two human beings are alike, yet each is a manifestation of God.

Your sense of exile is not a punishment but a misreading of the gift of uniqueness. It is through you and your uniqueness that God manifests and experiences the vast diversity of life. This diversity need not be at the expense of a higher unity, however.

Unity and diversity are both givens. The challenge is to see the latter as a manifestation of the former. The answer to human diversity is not human uniformity; we are not richer for being less creative. The answer to human diversity is to see that it is rooted in Divine Unity. Your very sense of exile comes from the One from Whom you cannot be in exile.

☐ Salvation Now

Reb Yisrael of Ruzhin once taught: "This is the prayer of my teacher, Rabbi Dov Ber of Mezritch: '*Ribbono shel Olam!*[1] Your people have suffered such a long exile! And why? Only because of stubbornness—Yours and ours! We have a long-standing argument, You and us.

"We say to You, 'Return us O God unto You, and we shall return!' You say to us, 'Return to Me, and I will return to you.'[2] And because of this mutual stubbornness You withhold our Redemption. Well, You have told us to follow Your ways. If You won't budge, we won't budge. This I swear to You: The Children of Israel will not return until Redemption!"

Reb Yisrael then added, "I agree with my teacher that we will not repent until the Messiah comes because we have a legitimate claim against God. And I suspect God will not send the Messiah until we first repent because God has a legitimate claim against us. But there is a way out of this impasse.

"We read in our siddur,[3] 'Because of our sins we were exiled from our land.' If this is true, then we should return to God before God returns to us. But the Hebrew word 'because' can also mean 'before,' and thus the prayer might say, 'Before we sinned we were already fated for exile.' Therefore, *Ribbono shel Olam*, just as You condemned us to exile before we sinned, You should now redeem us from exile before we repent!"

1 Deeds, words, and thoughts are called the Three Garments of the Soul, the three primary ways in which consciousness manifests in the world of human beings. The soul is pure and at one with God, but the Garments are stained by selfishness. Cleanse the Garments, and unity of all with All is apparent.

@ There are three levels of reality—physical, psychological, and spiritual—and each has its core epistemological principle. The German physicist Werner Heisenberg proved that at the deepest levels of physical world, we know nothing for certain. Every act of investigation colors that which we are investigating, and even math becomes metaphor. The Baal Shem Tov provides us with the principle governing knowledge in the psychological dimension: Everything we encounter is colored by the quality of our thoughts. God provides us with the third principle: "Be still and know" (Psalm 46:10). When you stop investigating, when you stop reacting, when you stop doing, then there is a knowing that surpasses all self-centered understanding. This knowing comes not from you but through you from God.

Reb David knew that before Reb Yitzchak could engage his wife constructively, he would have to let go of his own view of the situation. He would have to realize that he did not know the whole story and that his sense of justice was colored by his lack of knowledge. Acting and reacting from partiality makes it impossible to be an impartial mediator.

The same is true of you. To engage the world constructively, you have to cleanse your thoughts of partiality; you have to stop acting and reacting from your own limited knowledge; you have to be still and allow what is to be present without bias. Don't investigate, don't think, just receive, and then you will know how best to respond.

☐ Ask Yourself

When Reb Yitzchak of Vorki was a new husband, his wife complained about him every chance she got. Reb Yitzchak chose to endure her insults in silence. When he saw that she treated the servants in the same manner, he went to his rebbe, Reb David of Lelov, for advice.

The rebbe listened and said, "Why are you asking me? Ask yourself!"

Reb Yitzchak was confused by his teacher's response. He knew his teacher was trying to teach him something, but he was unsure as to what it was. Then he recalled a teaching of the Baal Shem Tov:

"If you suffer from the anguish of servants, it is due to your own error in action. If your spouse curses you, it is because you have failed to master your tongue. If your children trouble you, it is due to your obsession with errant thoughts. If you align these three[1] with godliness—if your thought, word, and deed are holy and hallowing—then all this distress turns to joy."

Suddenly Reb Yitzchak understood what his teacher was saying. If he wanted to improve the situation of others he must begin with himself.

1 *Eliyahu haNavi:* Elijah the Prophet.

2 2 Kings 1:8.

@ You are not your body—which is not to say that your body is not you. Your body is to you the way an apple is to an apple tree. It is part of the "treeing" process, just not the whole of it. To the extent that you identify with your body, you are fearful of your mortality. To the extent that you reject the body, you are fearful of your physical hungers. The balance point is to honor the body without being attached to the body.

You are not your feelings—which is not to say that your feelings are not you. Your feelings are to you the way clouds are to the sky. Clouds appear in the sky but are not confused with the sky. To the extent that you identify with your feelings, you are trapped on a roller coaster of mood swings. To the extent that you reject your feelings, you are fearful of every mood. The balance point is to feel your feelings without being attached to them.

You are not your thoughts—which is not to say that your thoughts are not you. Your thoughts are to you the way a chord is to a guitar. Pluck the strings, and a chord sounds; stimulate the mind, and thoughts appear. To the extent that you identify with your thoughts, you are trapped in your own creativity. To the extent that you reject your thoughts, you are trapped in ignorance. The balance point is to honor thinking without being attached to the thoughts.

Music is a way to let go of all this. To surrender to a repetitive chant, an ecstatic *niggun* (Hasidic melody), or a Bach fugue is to remove the belt and discover your true self.

☐ A Leather Belt

A certain Hasid once visited Reb Uri of Strelisk to complain about the behavior of Reb Yisrael of Ruzhin. According to this Hasid, Reb Yisrael would hire musicians to perform for him in private—an act of conceit this Hasid found highly distasteful.

Reb Uri asked the man to describe Reb Yisrael's state of mind when he listened to these musicians. What he heard was a portrait of a man transported into pure ecstasy.

"Do you know," asked the rebbe, "the meaning of the teaching regarding *Eliyahu haNavi*[1] that 'the girdle of his loins was a girdle of leather'?"[2]

"No," said the Hasid. "I do not."

"The meaning is this: The 'girdle of leather' means his flesh and blood. Eliyahu had the power to put on and take off this girdle at will. He could wear his physical body like a leather belt, putting it on and taking it off whenever he wished."

Not understanding the connection between Reb Yisrael and the Prophet Elijah, the Hasid stared blankly at his teacher.

Reb Uri sighed and said, "Reb Yisrael is like the Prophet. He can enter and leave his body at will. Music is his means for doing so."

1 *Rav:* Rabbinic leader.

2 *Yechidus* (from Hebrew for "unity"): The spiritual direction of a Hasid by the rebbe. The word suggests that the rebbe merges with the soul of the Hasid to see where, in this life or a past life, some misalignment with God has occurred. The rebbe then returns to the world of seeming duality and instructs the Hasid on how to repair the relationship with the Divine.

@ True meeting with another requires you to strip away the self; otherwise all you see is your own projection. *Yechidus* is this profound stripping away. Reb Shmuel, however, is sharing with us only the rebbe's side of *yechidus.* If the rebbe is to dress in the Hasid's clothes, the Hasid must be willing to stand naked to his or her situation. This is, of course, metaphor. The clothes are our conditioned thoughts, words, and deeds by which we define ourselves, and they, in turn, create the reality we encounter. Both the rebbe and the Hasid must see clearly how we condition our reality to reinforce the fit of the clothes we wear.

The rebbe learns what it is to be this Hasid, and the Hasid learns what it is to confront the world without clothes, without habits of thought, word, and deed. When the rebbe returns the clothes to the Hasid, he is inviting the Hasid to see things from this new perspective. And, since the rebbe knows the inner life of the Hasid, he can help him do just that.

☐ Hard Work

Reb David Chein, the *rav*[1] of Chernigov, was late for his *yechidus*[2] with his rebbe, Reb Shmuel of Lubavitch. Not wanting to bother the rebbe unduly, he thought to wait in the room next to the rebbe's study and ask his question when the rebbe was through with his last interview. The rebbe's assistant soon joined him, carrying a fresh change of clothes.

The attendant nodded to the clothes he was holding and said, "I don't understand why he needs to change after *yechidus*. And yet, when he comes out, the rebbe is dripping with perspiration. The entire period is but a single hour, and the rebbe sits at his desk the whole time. I mean, he doesn't move or do anything physical, and yet he sweats as if he were a laborer. After all," the attendant said sarcastically, "it isn't as if *yechidus* is such hard work!"

Just then the rebbe opened his door. Looking straight at the attendant, he said, "Your services are no longer needed. Please go home. I will have your wages delivered to you there."

Stunned, the attendant handed the rebbe his clothes, turned, and quickly walked away.

"Do you want to know why I perspire so?" the rebbe called after him. Red-faced, the man turned and said sheepishly, "Yes, Rebbe, I do."

"Over the past hour I have received twenty-five Hasidim for *yechidus*. If I am to understand each person's situation, I must divest myself of my clothes and dress myself in his. If I am to give him good advice, I must remove his clothes and change back into mine, for while in his clothes I can see only what he sees, and if he saw a way out of his dilemma he would not have come to me in the first place. So for the past hour I have undressed and dressed myself fifty times. It is very hard work!"

1   *Misnagedim:* The opponents of the Hasidim.

2   Minyan: Prayer quorum of ten.

3   *Tallis:* A four-cornered fringed shawl worn during certain prayers as a reminder of God's Presence (Numbers 15:38).

4   *Tefillin* ("phylacteries"): Two small black leather boxes containing four passages from Torah: Exodus 13:1–10, 11–16; Deuteronomy 6:4–9, 13–21.

5   *Mishnayos:* The Mishnah (teaching, instruction) is the first authoritative collection of rabbinic teaching spanning the period from 250 B.C.E. to 250 C.E.

6   The sacrifices stopped with the destruction of the Temple in 70 C.E.

☐ Fooling the Evil Inclination

On a trip through Ruzhin, a group of *misnagedim*[1] thought to visit Reb Yisrael to complain about the behavior of his Hasidim.

"You call us antagonists, but at least we walk in the path of God. We study Torah at set times, we pray with a minyan[2] each morning, and when we are finished with our prayers we sit in our *tallis*[3] and *tefillin*[4] and study *Mishnayos*.[5] But you Hasidim who dare to call yourselves the pious ones pray when you feel like it, and then sit down to a glass of vodka! Why, it is outrageous to call this piety!"

The rebbe listened to their complaint quietly. When they were finished, he said, "My learned guests, as you well know, the times of prayer were set to correspond to the sacrifices in the Temple, which can no longer be performed.[6] As you also know, an improper thought in the mind can render both sacrifice and prayer unclean. So we wait to pray until our minds are clear of distractions."

The *misnagedim* were impressed with this answer. "And the drinking after prayer?"

(continued on page 99)

7 Evil Inclination (Hebrew: *yetzer harah*): People are born with two innate passions: the passion for self-effacement (*yetzer hatov,* the Good Inclination) and the passion for self-aggrandizement, the Evil Inclination. The latter can be channeled to serve the former, creating a balance between self-care and service to others.

8 *L'Chayyim* ("To Life!"): Traditional toast when drinking.

9 *Mamaloshen:* Mother tongue, referring to Yiddish—the everyday language of Eastern European Jews from the early Middle Ages to the present.

@ True prayer is the spontaneous outpouring of an open and naked soul. Such prayer cannot be controlled, edited, or fixed, and yet this is precisely what the Evil Inclination urges us to do. It haunts us with the notion that only the old words, the formal words, the words of the past, can reach God, the Eternal Present. It offers us an image of God as habit, a God that is reduced to fixed forms and formulae. Reb Yisrael offers us another view: God as unscripted Presence-in-Life. Therefore the only true prayer is *L'Chayyim*: To Life!

"As you no doubt also know, the Evil Inclination[7] is the source of these thoughts and has invented many strategies for distracting us. So we Hasidim have a counter-strategy. After formal prayer, we sit and wish each other '*L'Chayyim!*'[8] At that moment, each of us in turn reveals to the group his most desperate need, and we respond 'May God grant your request!' Now the Evil Inclination is listening to all of this, but since it is said in an informal way, in *mamaloshen*[9] rather than Hebrew, the Evil One assumes we are speaking idly and ignores us. Yet, Torah tells us that prayer can be in any language, so our seemingly informal talk is in fact the deepest prayer, untainted by distracting thoughts and certain to rise all the way to heaven."

Not knowing how to respond, the *misnagedim* nodded curtly to the rebbe and returned to their journey.

1 *Talmid chacham* (literally, "wise student"): Scholar.

@ What are the thoughts that haunt you? Most likely they are legion. Yet, they probably all have one thing in common: They are thoughts of dissatisfaction. Things are simply not the way you wish them to be. Are these alien thoughts? Not at all. They are your everyday musings.

What our Hasid desires is to clear his mind of these thoughts. Can you do this? Or is the thought of a clear mind yet another variation of the same thought that always haunts you: "I am dissatisfied"?

There is only one way to deal with these thoughts: Let them be. If you try to rid yourself of "alien thoughts," you are only adding more dissatisfaction to your life. If you try to change your mind during prayer, you will only add to the conflict that muddies the mind and makes prayer difficult.

So what can you do? "Commune with your heart and be still" (Psalm 4:5). To commune with your heart is to be present to the thoughts and feelings that arise. Notice them, but don't engage them. That is what it is to "be still." Don't move; don't run after the thought to investigate it or change it. Simply note it, and let it be.

And do not think that in this way you will be rid of such thoughts. The goal isn't to be rid of anything but to be present to everything. What you will discover in stillness is not the end of such thoughts but your capacity to hold them without having them take hold of you. You are like the sky making room for clouds and yet not being attached to cloudiness. This is true prayer: communing with our hearts in stillness.

☐ Alien Invaders

A Hasid once visited the *Chozeh* of Lublin, Reb Yaakov Yitzchak, to complain of alien thoughts that would invade his mind and make prayer impossible for him.

"And what thoughts trouble you?" the Seer asked.

The man then went on to catalog a great list of thoughts: His business was not as good as it could be, his customers owed him too much, his competitors were undermining his profits, his wife was not satisfied with their livelihood, his daughters needed dowries, his son was not the *talmid chacham*[1] he had prayed for, and on and on.

When he had finished, the *Chozeh* said, "Alien thoughts? My dear friend, these are not alien thoughts at all. Why, they are clearly thoughts that are quite at home in your mind!"

1 *Mikveh* (literally, "a gathering place of water"): Ritual bath. Along with the synagogue and *beis midrash* (religion school), the *mikveh* has been a central institution of Jewish communal life since ancient times. First mentioned in Leviticus 11:36 as a means for purifying people and utensils, the *mikveh* was used by the Hasidim as a means of cleansing themselves of impure and selfish thoughts before Shabbat.

ℯ Here are two paths to enlightenment. The way of Dov Ber's father takes us on an arduous journey of self-discipline, slowly stripping away the stains that sully the window through which the pure light of God is streaming. The second is way of Reb Zusya: opening the window without cleaning it, allowing the light to flood in and bathe you in pure divine ecstasy. There are value and danger in both paths.

If you clean the window, the value is the purifying of your character that prepares you to receive the Divine Light and use it for the good. The danger is that you will obsess over every stain and never experience the Light. If you open the window, the value is the immediate experience of bliss. The danger is that you have not prepared your character to receive it and cannot use it for anything but self-aggrandizement.

Perhaps for most of us, the best way is a blending of these two paths. Cleanse the window while it is open; experience the Presence of God and use that experience to cleanse the self of selfishness.

There is, however, a third path: throw a brick through the window, and shatter the glass once and for all. Just remember to clean up the mess afterward.

☐ Salvation through Joy

A wedding party once passed by the home of Reb Zusya of Hanipoli. The rebbe raced outdoors and danced before the bride and groom with joyous abandon. When he returned indoors, his family was waiting for him, scowling. "It is unseemly for the rebbe of Hanipoli to dance at some strangers' wedding," they said.

Reb Zusya smiled and said, "I will tell you a story: Once, when I was a young student, my rebbe scolded me severely. He later asked my forgiveness, which, of course, I was eager to give. But that night the ghost of his father awakened me, saying, 'I have but one son left on this earth, and you would destroy him because he criticized you?'

"I explained that I had indeed forgiven him, but the ghost said, 'You do not know the meaning of forgiveness.' In an instant he transported me to the *mikveh*[1]. 'Immerse yourself three times,' the ghost said, 'and each time affirm that you have forgiven my son.' I did as I was told, and when I came out of the *mikveh*, the ghost shone with the light of the noonday sun.

"Seeing my amazement, the rebbe said, 'This light is my true face. It comes in fulfillment of three rules: honoring others, forgiving others, and being generous toward others. You honor and are generous, but you could not see it until you had experienced the joy of complete forgiveness.'"

Reb Zusya paused for a moment, and his wife said, "And what does all of this have to do with my husband dancing like a madman at those strangers' wedding?"

"Ah, yes!" Reb Zusya continued. "What my rebbe's father had attained through his three laws, I attain through pure joy. It is joy that reveals our true nature! So when I saw the wedding party, I remembered this teaching and raced outside to participate fully in the principle of joy!"

1 *Rebbitzin:* The wife of a rabbi.

2 *Shabbos:* The Sabbath. It is customary to wear one's finer clothes on the Sabbath as a sign of respect for the day.

3 *Kallah:* Bride.

4 *Tzedakah:* Generosity, from the Hebrew *tzedek,* "justice." Every Jew is obligated to give 10 percent of his or her earnings to help the needy. It is customary to do this with the week's earnings before Shabbat. Hasidic rebbes and *rebbitzins* were often noted for giving all their money away before Shabbat.

☐ The Tailor's Due

One day, Reb Zusyah of Hanipoli found his *rebbitzin*[1] crying softly. "What is the matter?" he asked. She hesitated to say, but at his urging she told him that even her finest dress was tattered and frayed and could no longer honor the *Shabbos*[2] as it had done for so many years. Understanding her desire to honor the *Shabbos*, the rebbe raised the money and bought the cloth for a new dress. She was delighted and took it to the tailor, who promised her it would be ready Friday afternoon, hours before the start of the Sabbath.

That Friday afternoon, the rebbe expected to see his wife aglow with the joy of honoring the *Shabbos* in her new dress, but instead he found her wearing the old dress. Seeing his surprise, she said, "The tailor himself came by with the dress. It was exquisite. But he looked very distressed. I asked him what troubled him, and he told me that his future son-in-law had seen him working on my dress and assumed it was for his daughter's wedding. He even went so far as to tell his *kallah*[3] the good news. Oy, what could I do? If the girl found out the dress was not for her, she would be so disappointed, and her father so ashamed, so I gave the tailor the dress as a gift for his daughter's wedding."

"And did you pay him?" the rebbe asked.

"Pay him? Why no, I gave him the dress."

"As a gift, you gave it to him. All week long he anticipated payment. Now we have robbed him of his due."

"You are right," the *rebbitzin* said, "but I have given all our money to *tzedakah*."[4]

(continued on page 107)

@ What are your obligations to others?

There are two kinds of people who argue that you have no obligations to others. The first argues from the absolute: There is no "other," and therefore nothing to be done. The second argues from the relative: We must work out our own fate by ourselves.

There are two kinds of people who argue that you are obligated to others. The first argues from the absolute: God is the other and thus must be honored. The second argues from the relative: Do unto others as you would want them to do unto you.

Reb Zusyah and his wife show you another way: "If I am not for myself, who will be for me? But, if I am only for myself, what [kind of a person] am I? And if not now, when?" (*Pirke Avot* 1:14). Right now, you must be for self and other. This is the way of the Hasidim. Self and other are both real, but neither is separate from the other. Each moment you are asked to find a path of action that honors both self and other. How do you respond to that call?

"Then we must raise more," Reb Zusya said, "and quickly, for it is almost *Shabbos.*"

The *rebbitzin* then raced out of the house, borrowed the money from a friend, and paid the tailor for his work just before *Shabbos.*

1 *Klee Elohim:* (literally, "a godly vessel"): One who is required to free the self from all personal likes and dislikes, following only the will of God and erasing all traces of self and selfishness.

@ Can you ever love your neighbor as you love yourself (Leviticus 19:18)? Or, more importantly, would you want to? Reb Menachem Mendel thought it could be done and must be done. He wanted his heart opened so wide as to embrace even strangers as his own kin. And yet, he couldn't do so. He saw this as a failure, but would we?

On the contrary, we love in concentric circles. We begin with ourselves. If we can truly love, honor, and respect ourselves, then we can do the same for others. The first "other" is our family; then our spouse, partner, and children; then our community; then our ethnic group; then all people; then all beings; then the world as a whole. But these loves are not equal in passion. I will never love a stranger's son as I love my own, but I can nevertheless know how to treat him with honor and respect because I have learned from doing so with my own.

Menachem Mendel thought that you must love everyone the same. He is wrong. To love someone is to love what is unique about that person. Love is not a one-size-fits-all emotion. It is truest when it is unique to the person being loved. Indeed, a one-size-fits-all love threatens to erase the very things that make each person valuable.

Love people differently, just love them all.

☐ The Rebbe's Love

Sarah, the daughter of Reb Menachem Mendel of Vizhnitz, lived with her husband in his father's home in Belz. It happened that she fell ill, and to keep her father informed the son-in-law sent daily telegrams to Reb Menachem Mendel to update him on her status.

One day no telegram arrived, and the rebbe became very distressed. His son, Reb Baruch, tried to comfort him. "It is still not too late for a telegram to arrive," he said. "There is probably some holdup with the deliveries." Several hours later, a telegram did arrive, informing the rebbe that his daughter had made a full recovery.

Reb Baruch heard this and went to rejoice with his father. Expecting to find the rebbe relieved, he was shocked to find his father weeping.

"I don't understand," he said. "Sarah is fine, thank God, and you are not consoled?"

The rebbe said, "Trait by trait I have purified my character in order to make myself a pure *klee Elohim*.[1] But there was one trait that I found almost impossible to master: loving my neighbor as myself. I had finally arrived at a state where I could love all people as I love your sister, you, and myself. All week long I receive letters and telegrams telling me of the pain and suffering of my neighbors, and yet this one telegram is late and I react not as a rebbe but as a father. I still love you more than them. And for this I am quite sad."

Alter Rebbe (literally, "The Old Rebbe"): Term of endearment applied to the founder of HaBaD, Reb Shneur Zalman.

@ Was the Alter Rebbe crying because he had not read the book or because his son had not read it? We can assume that if Reb Shneur Zalman was willing for his son to risk the ban of Rabbeinu Gershom, he himself had already done so. Yet, if he knew what was in the book, could he not simply teach his son, even though the book itself was gone?

The Alter Rebbe was not crying over a book. He was crying over his son's unwillingness to risk everything for wisdom. Wisdom is worth every sacrifice. Look carefully at the story of Eve in the Garden of Eden: "When the woman saw that the tree was good for eating and a delight to the eyes, and that the tree was desirable as a source of wisdom, she took of its fruit and ate. She also gave some to her husband, and he ate" (Genesis 3:6).

Unlike her husband, Eve did not simply take of the fruit and eat. She thought about it long and hard. First, she saw that the tree was good for eating; that is, she saw that it would ease her hunger. But that was not enough to make her violate the ban against eating it. Second, she realized that the fruit was beautiful, that it satisfied her craving for the aesthetic. But that, too, was not enough to motivate her to violate God's decree. Only when she saw that the fruit would make her wise did she take and eat it. It was not hunger, desire, or passion but wisdom alone that motivated her. She was willing to risk death for wisdom, and we should do no less.

☐ The Value of Wisdom

Reb Shneur Zalman of Liadi had a great library of sacred texts and teachings. Among his books was a rare manuscript of Hasidic philosophy. On the cover of the book was the following inscription: "The ban of Rabbeinu Gershom respecting the secrecy of documents is hereby invoked—in This World and the Next."

It once happened that a fire broke out in the rebbe's home, destroying all his books and manuscripts. The Alter Rebbe[1] called his son, Reb Dov Ber of Lubavitch, to his side.

"Did you ever open this book?" he asked, tears stinging his eyes.

"No, father, not once."

"Perhaps you were curious and opened it. Read a chapter or two. Can you recall a chapter of this manuscript? Even a single discourse from this book would restore my spirits."

Astonished, Reb Dov Ber said: "But father, the ban of Rabbeinu Gershom clearly states that one who opens this manuscript will be cursed in This World and the Next."

"And you didn't think that the discovery of some new wisdom was worth the sacrifice?"

1 *Cheder*: Elementary school.

2 *Melamed*: Tutor.

3 Lag b'Omer: The thirty-third day (*lag* in Hebrew) of the Counting of the Omer. The *omer* (sheaf) is an offering of new barley brought to the Temple on the second day of Passover. Rabbinic custom is to count fifty days beginning with the second day of Passover to the holy day of Shavuot, the anniversary of the giving of the Ten Commandments on Mount Sinai. This period is marked as a time of serious introspection as we move from Egypt to Sinai, from slavery to freedom. The thirty-third day of Omer, however, is set aside as a day of rejoicing and is often celebrated with picnics and bonfires.

℮ Menachem Mendel's love of God revealed to him even as a boy that creation was God manifest. Heaven and earth, the sacred and the mundane, the One and the many are all God. God is not an abstraction, an idea. God is the Source and substance of all reality. God is embraced not in some ethereal realm, but here and now in the birthing and dying of the natural world. Menachem Mendel was a rebbe because he saw God everywhere as everything, and he did not refrain from embracing the One as the many.

The Making of a Rebbe

Several Hasidim of Reb Menachem Mendel of Kotsk were visiting the town of Tomashov, singing the praises of their teacher. One of the townspeople was stunned by the news that Menachem Mendel was a rebbe.

"Why, he and I were classmates! We went to *cheder*[1] together as young children! A rebbe! How marvelous!"

Learning that they had a boyhood friend of their rebbe's in their midst, the Hasidim pestered him for information about Menachem Mendel as a young man. The man insisted there was nothing to tell, nothing special about his friend. He was a boy like all others, the man insisted.

Just as the Hasidim were about to take leave of the man, he said: "No, wait! I do remember something. Once our *melamed*[2] took us all out to celebrate Lag b'Omer[3] with a picnic held high in the mountains beyond Tomashov. After the picnic, we all returned home together. All, that is, but Menachem Mendel. He was no longer among us.

"We raced back up the mountain and found him lying face down on the mountainside, his arms and legs outstretched as far as they could go. He was hugging the mountain with all his might and speaking directly to the earth.

"Our teacher went over to him and listened to what he was saying. He heard Menachem Mendel repeating the phrase 'My heart and my flesh sing praises to the living God' over and over and over again."

1 Torah, *avodah, mitzvos:* "Torah" refers to the written and oral teachings found in the Bible and Talmud. *Avodah* refers to the three-times-a-day worship service. *Mitzvos* are the commandments revealed by God and interpreted by the Rabbis.

@ Does this mean that Reb Elimelech avoided Torah study, prayed half-heartedly, and ignored the commandments? Not at all. It just means that he realized he had never reached his full potential regarding any of these things. This realization could have driven him to despair. He could have felt himself unworthy of heaven, and driven himself mad with self-flagellation. To do so would have meant that heaven can be earned and that Reb Elimelech simply failed to measure up. But he knew differently: You cannot earn your way into heaven. All you can be is honest with and about yourself.

Reb Elimelech knew the truth of *dayyenu,* enough. There is always another page of Talmud to study; there is always a deeper level of spiritual awareness open to us in prayer; there is always another act of kindness to seek out and do; but we cannot do everything. We must only do enough.

What is enough? Only you know that. Reb Elimelech, however, gives a hint. He answers the judges of the heavenly court without remorse. He doesn't deny or defend his life; he simply accepts it. When you can do the same, you have reached *dayyenu.*

Wouldn't that excuse laziness and even immorality? If you are looking for an excuse, you are not accepting what is. If your claim to *dayyenu* is false, meaning that you did not do all you could given your circumstances, then honesty, humility, and grace are lost. Without these, there is no way into this world or the World to Come.

☐ Without a Doubt

His Hasidim asked Reb Elimelech of Lyzhansk if he were certain that he was assured a place in the World to Come.

"Absolutely," the rebbe replied without hesitation.

"And how, Rebbe, can you be so certain?"

"When we die in this world, we go before the heavenly court in the World Above. Standing before the divine court, we are asked certain questions regarding Torah, *avodah*, and *mitzvos*.[1] Answer these properly, and you will go to the World to Come."

"And you know these questions, Rebbe?" the students asked.

"Yes."

"And you know the answers?"

"Yes."

"And will you share them with us?"

"The questions are the same for all of us. Your answers must be your own. Yet, I will tell you just what I will tell them. They will ask: 'Rebbe, did you study Torah to the best of your ability?' And I will answer honestly: 'No.' They will then ask: 'Rebbe, did you fully surrender to God in worship?' And I will answer honestly: 'No.' They will then ask me: 'Rebbe, did you do the *mitzvos* and good deeds you could do while alive?' And I will answer honestly: 'No.' And then they will say: 'If so, then you are telling us the truth, and for that alone are you welcome into the World to Come.'"

1 *Yiddin:* Yiddish for Jews.

2 *Alef-beis:* The Hebrew alphabet.

3 *Yud:* The tenth letter of the Hebrew alphabet. A *yud* looks like this: **'**.

4 *Melamed:* Tutor.

5 The Holy Name of God: The four-letter Name YHVH, referring to God as all He was, is, and will ever be. The Name is often referred to by an abbreviation of two *yuds.*

6 *Chumash:* The Five Books of Moses, from the Hebrew *chamesh,* five.

@ The *yud* is the smallest letter of the Hebrew alphabet. It is nothing but a dot. Yet, two *yuds* together point to the One Who is all. By yourself you are nothing, a mere speck on the face of the planet. But when you sit together with another in real meeting, the two of you are everything. Why? Because true meeting requires the recognition of another as an equal. If you seek to raise the other above yourself, or raise yourself above the other, there is no real meeting. God is present between self and other when each regards the other as an equal.

☐ Two Yids, Two Yuds

Once, the Yid HaKodesh asked his Hasidim, "How is it that if two
Yiddin[1] sit together and neither seeks to elevate himself over the other,
God forgives them all their sins?"

Hearing no reply, the Holy Jew told this story: "When I was a
young child first learning the alef-beis,[2] I pointed to the letter yud[3] and
asked my melamed,[4] 'What is this dot?'

"My teacher said, 'It is the letter yud.'

"I then pointed to two yuds together and said, 'What shall I make of
these two dots together?'

"'These two yuds together,' he told me, 'spell out the Holy Name of
God.'[5]

"I was fascinated, and looked very carefully in the Chumash[6] to find
these two dots, these two yuds that were the Name of God. As I did so
I came across two other dots, one stacked on top of the other. 'What is
this?' I asked.

"'That is called a colon,' my teacher told me.

"'These dots look like those dots,' I said. 'How will I remember the
difference?'

"'Easily,' he said. 'When the two dots sit next to each other as equals,
they are the Name of God. When one lords it over the other, then they
are not the Name of God.'

"From this I learned that when two yids sit next to each other as
equals, they form the Name of God and are forgiven all their faults. But
when you seek to raise yourself over another, then you are not the Name
of God, and no forgiveness happens."

1 Reb Levi Yitzchak of Berditchev (1740–1810).

2 Reb Shmelke of Nikilsburg (1726–1778): Hasid of Dov Ber of Mezritch, who focused on generosity as the center of his spiritual life.

3 *Nu:* Yiddish expression for "So?"

℮ What do you know? What do you know the way you know you are hungry after a long fast? It is this kind of knowing that Reb Levi Yitzchak experienced at the rabbinic court of Shmelke of Nikolsburg. It is this kind of knowing—a firsthand kind of knowing—that is at the heart of true spiritual awakening.

Too often we make do with secondhand knowing. We mistake concepts for truth. We know that God is one, but we do not experience oneness. We know that God is love, but we do not experience compassion. We know that God is good, but we do not experience goodness. We know that God is just, but we do not experience justice.

We are filled with a secondhand knowing; we master the menu and never eat the meal; we worship the map and never walk the territory. It is not hard to be filled with such knowledge. Even the maid knows what we know, for she, no less than we, has been brought up on the same menu.

When the Israelites received the Torah at Mount Sinai they said, "*Na'aseh v'nishmah:* We will do and we will hear" (Exodus 24:7). You would expect the order to be reversed: We hear first, and then do. But the deeper hearing, the deeper understanding, can come only from doing. Experience is the teacher; life is the rebbe.

Nu?

☐ Knowing

When Reb Levi Yitzchak of Berditchev[1] returned home from his first visit to his rebbe, Reb Shmelke of Nikolsburg,[2] his father-in-law said, "And what did you learn there that you could not learn here?"

"I learned that there is a Creator of the universe," Reb Levi Yitzchak replied.

"And for that you had to travel to Nikolsburg?" He then called to his maid and asked her, "What do you say? Is there a Creator of the universe?"

"Of course!" she said.

"Nu?"[3] Reb Levi Yitzchak's father-in-law said.

Reb Levi Yitzchak responded, "She says, I know."

1 Bar mitzvah (literally, "master of the commandment"): A Jewish boy (bat mitzvah is the contemporary equivalent for girls) who has reached the age of legal maturity, age thirteen, when he is responsible for all the ritual obligations and is held accountable for all his deeds.

2/3 *Yetzer hatov/Yetzer harah:* People are born with two inclinations or passions: *yetzer hatov,* the inclination for goodness, and *yetzer harah,* the inclination for evil. Without these inclinations, people could not become free agents, making moral choices about the quality of life and how to live it.

ℯ The *yetzer hatov,* the inclination to selflessness, sets the direction of your heart. It points not *to* the self but *through* the self to the greater ground out of which the self arises. The *yetzer harah,* the inclination for selfishness, grounds you in the immediacy of your situation. The early Rabbis taught that without the *yetzer harah* you would not build a business or raise a family. Without the grounding in this world that the *yetzer harah* provides, you would ignore this world and get caught up in the ethereal.

Allow the *yetzer harah* to ground you in your situation. Respect your desires, and celebrate your gifts. Allow the *yetzer hatov* to direct your desires and gifts toward the greater good, the good that honors both self and other, person and planet. The goal is not to align yourself with one or the other of these inclinations but to align them with each other and to use them both.

☐ Partners

The day before becoming bar mitzvah,[1] Reb Yisrael of Ruzhin was called into his father's study. His father, Reb Shalom Shachna Friedmann, said to him: "Tomorrow, my son, you will receive a very special visitor, one who will not leave you for the rest of your life. Are you prepared to welcome this guest lovingly, as befits one of her stature?"

"Yes, father. This guest is the *yetzer hatov*,[2] the passion for selflessness, goodness, kindness, and compassion. I began to prepare for her arrival long ago."

"Really!" Reb Shalom Simcha said. "And when was that?"

"When her partner, the *yetzer harah*,[3] the passion for selfishness, came to join me. I received her respectfully and said: 'You know that you and the *yetzer hatov* are partners. You both dwell together in every heart. It would be unseemly of me to welcome one partner without the other.'

"So I convinced the *yetzer harah* to leave and return only with the *yetzer hatov*. So in this way I am prepared to welcome them both into my heart together!"

1 *Shacharit:* The morning prayer service, derived from the Hebrew word *shachar,* dawn. The morning service is the longest of the three daily services and consists of five parts: Morning Benedictions, Songs of Praise, Summons to Prayer, Affirmation of God's Unity and the Centrality of Love, and the Eighteen Prayers of Petition.

ℚ How are you to judge the spiritual quality of a saint? How are you to know whether your rebbe or teacher is truly wise or simply but brilliantly insane? This is Reb Asher's problem. He married into the household of Reb Naftali, a rebbe whose reputation as an affable guide and mentor was known throughout the Hasidic world. And yet, here is his father-in-law seemingly scolding the servants for something as minor as milk.

Reb Asher's first inclination is to call his father-in-law to account for his behavior, but when he sees how kindly Reb Naftali treats the needy, he forgets the harshness of a moment ago. In time, Reb Asher comes to see that his father-in-law is not complaining to the servants at all, but to God. It is to God that he makes his demands for milk, that the babies might be nourished and grow strong.

This is the rebbe's job: to call God to account. The rebbe and God are friends, and the role of a friend is to hold up a mirror to the other that she might see the mistakes she makes and correct them. The rebbe holds up a mirror to God: the dry breast, the watery milk. He says to his Friend in the strongest terms: This is not right; You can do better.

Sometimes the rebbe speaks to God as God; sometimes the rebbe speaks to God as you. When your teacher challenges you, see whether the challenge is to be a better you. If it is, then you are in the presence of a saint. If it isn't, you may be in the presence of a madman.

122

☐ What I Deserve

Reb Asher had recently married the daughter of Reb Naftali of Ropshitz and had moved into the rebbe's house. One morning before *Shacharit,*[1] Reb Asher was appalled when his father-in-law stormed into the kitchen, where he was sitting with the women of the house, and called brusquely, "For all my efforts, don't I deserve a little milk?"

"This is no way to speak to people," Reb Asher said to himself. "I will have to speak to my father-in-law."

At that moment, a neighborhood woman came into the kitchen, crying. "Rebbe," she said to Reb Naftali, "my breasts are dry and I cannot nurse my twins!"

Reb Naftali spoke to her softly and said, "Go home and nurse your children. God will help you."

The plea of the neighbor caused Reb Asher to forget his vow to rebuke his father-in-law, but several weeks later he was again startled when the rebbe burst into the kitchen, bellowing: "So I get a little milk, but of such poor quality it does no good at all. Can it be that I do not deserve a bit of nourishing milk?"

Again Reb Asher was stunned at the harsh talk of his father-in-law. He recalled the prior event and was about to say something when the very same neighbor came into the kitchen. "Rebbe," she said. "The milk flowed, but now it is watery, and my children are weak and skinny like sticks. Please, Rebbe, pray to God that I be blessed with healthy milk!"

Reb Naftali again spoke to her, saying, "Go home and nurse. God will help you."

At this Reb Asher realized what his father-in-law had been doing, and he knew that he was a rebbe after all.

L'Chayyim: "To Life!" A classic Jewish toast.

Ribbono shel Olam: Master of the Universe, a common Yiddish appellation for God.

Nu: Yiddish expression for "So?"

@ How can it be that God either suffers or rejoices? Isn't God beyond such things? The answer to such questions depends, of course, on how you define God. If God is, as the Hasidim thought, the One Thing that manifests as all things, then God is not removed from joy or suffering. In fact, we are among the ways in which God experiences joy and suffering.

Just as a wave is the ocean manifest in a specific time and place, so you are God manifest in and of your unique situation. You are not, of course, all of God, but God is all of you. You are the way God raises your family, or walks your dog, or grooms your cat, or takes out the garbage. You are also the way God laughs and cries, celebrates and suffers. If God is all, then God is you. If God is you, and you know pleasure and pain, then God too—through you—knows pleasure and pain.

This is what Reb Fishel knew, and this is what he did about it. He sought to give God pleasure by doing something pleasurable. What a wonderful practice! Imagine that all you do either pleasures or pains God. Wouldn't you do your best to maximize the former and minimize the latter? Wouldn't you do your best to ensure that your actions are truly good and pleasurable and not merely expedient and titillating?

Follow the example of Reb Naftali, and find something to do each day that offers up pure pleasure to God. In this way you will spread joy throughout the world, for the more pleasure the world gives to God, the more pleasure the world receives from God.

☐ Good Night God

Reb Fishel of Strikov was known for a seemingly strange nighttime ritual. Every night before retiring to bed, the rebbe would pour himself a glass of vodka. He would say the blessing over the drink, take a sip from the glass, and then call aloud to God: "*L'Chayyim*,[1] *Ribbono shel Olam*,[2] Source of Life and Life of all the living! A very good night to You, *Ribbono shel Olam!*" And then he would wash the glass and go to sleep.

As this practice became more widely rumored, his Hasidim came to him for an explanation.

Reb Fishel said, "Is God afflicted by human suffering?"

"Yes," his students answered. "We are taught that God suffers when humans suffer."

"So," the rebbe said, "if God is pained by our pain, it stands to reason that God rejoices in our joy. Now if this is true, then if the suffering of the world were to have a night of peace, this would bring God a good night as well, yes?"

"Yes," his disciples said.

"*Nu*,[3] when I wish God a good night, there is then only one way in which He can arrange for this. He must give a night's rest and peace to all the afflicted of the world!"

1 Reb Dov Ber of Mezritch (1704 [?]–1772): Successor to the Baal Shem Tov, Dov Ber provided Hasidism with a formal theology derived from kabbalistic teaching. Called the *Maggid,* or Preacher, Dov Ber spoke primarily to his inner circle of Hasidim, focusing on levels of teaching that the average person could not fathom. Essential to Dov Ber's theology was the notion that God is the only reality, and all things are temporary manifestations of God.

@ What is the one act at the heart of the deepest faith? Is it self-effacement? Humility? Scrupulous adherence to the rituals of one's tradition? For Dov Ber, the one defining act of faith is generosity.

This rich and pious visitor saw his wealth as a test of his will. He could revel in his riches, but that would seem to suggest a lack of pious humility. So he did not live up to his means but instead took great pride in living well below them. In so doing, the merchant failed in several ways. First, he failed to enjoy the gifts life had bestowed upon him. In this he was ungrateful. Second, he failed to share his wealth with others. In this he was miserly. And third, he failed to realize the true nature of human service to God: being godly to others. In this he failed to love his neighbor as he loved himself. Or did he?

In fact, this wealthy merchant did love his neighbor as he loved himself. His problem was that he did not really love himself. Reb Dov Ber wanted this fellow to love himself so that he might love God and his neighbor. You are here to serve God by being godly toward your neighbor, the stranger, nature, and life itself. The gifts God gives you are to be shared.

The true lover of God is a lover of life and all the living. See what gifts you have been given, and honor them, rejoice in them, use them to the best of your ability. As you do, you will find a generosity of spirit that will open your heart and hand to share your gifts with others.

☐ Stone Soup

A wealthy merchant once visited Reb Dov Ber, the *Maggid* of Mezritch.[1] He joined the rebbe and his Hasidim for a light meal.

"Tell me," said the *Maggid*, "given your wealth and piety, what does a man such as yourself eat?"

The man was flattered that the *Maggid* referenced not only his wealth but also his devotion to this faith. After all, he worked hard at achieving both.

"Well, Rebbe," the man said with great pride, "I could accustom myself to the finest foods, but I fear these would tempt me toward worldliness. So I make do with the diet of the poor: a slice of bread and a pinch of salt."

"How dare you defame the Creator this way!" the *Maggid* cried. "You have been blessed with wealth and power, and yet you deny the legitimate pleasures that come with it. This is an insult to God, Who gave these things. From now on you are to eat meat and drink wine every day!"

The *Maggid*'s visitor was shocked; the *Maggid*'s Hasidim all the more so. When the man left, they begged their rebbe to explain his outburst. Obviously, this man was doing his best to free himself of the temptations of this world, and the *Maggid* had rebuked him for it.

"Perhaps," the *Maggid* replied. "But I will tell you this: If this wealthy fellow grows accustomed to eating meat and drinking wine, he will certainly realize that the poor need to eat at least bread and salt. But if he, a rich man, can make do with bread and salt, then he will surmise that the poor can survive on water and stones."

1 *Beis midrash* (literally, "House of Study"): A communally run center for religious learning where young men would spend the entire day poring over the Bible and Talmud. Today, such centers are usually privately run.

2 *Tzitzis* ("fringes;" modern Hebrew, *tzitzit* or *arbah kanfot,* four corners, or *tallit katan,* small prayer shawl): A four-cornered fringed undergarment worn by observant Jews in fulfillment of the commandment "They shall make for themselves fringes on the corners of their garments for all generations..." (Numbers 15:38). One is supposed to look upon the fringes and be reminded that one is always surrounded by the Presence of God. To be made visible, the *tzitzis* are worn long so they hang below one's clothes.

℮ Do you know the difference between earning a living and earning a livelihood? Many people don't. You don't earn your living; your living is a gift from God through your parents. Your livelihood must be earned, but what if earning your livelihood interferes with honoring the gift of your living? This is the question that troubles Reb Levi Yitzchak.

And how are you to know what your livelihood really is? In your scramble for money to pay your bills, could it be that you are missing opportunities not only for living, but for livelihood as well?

There is a tendency to mistake movement for living. If you keep busy, you must be living. The business magazine *Fast Company* has as its motto a quote from Hunter Thompson: "Faster and faster until the thrill of speed overcomes the fear of death." Levi Yitzchak wants us to slow down to the speed of life. What is that speed? When Jacob becomes Israel (the God Wrestler, or Spiritual Warrior), he reveals to his brother Esau, the conventional warrior, what the speed of life really is: "I will walk on gently according to the pace of the cattle and the nursing calves, and the gait of the children..." (Genesis 33:14). The speed of life is the pace of the nursing and the nursed. If you want to live well, slow down.

☐ Livelihood

On his way to the *beis midrash*,[1] Reb Levi Yitzchak of Berditchev saw a man racing across the market square. He ran so fast that his coattails and *tzitzis*[2] flapped behind him. In one hand he clutched a tattered brief-case; the other hand was clamped on top of his hat to keep it from fly-ing off his head. As the man ran past, Reb Levi Yitzchak called to him. The man stopped for a moment in deference to the rebbe, and greeted him between gulps of air.

"Where are you running to so swiftly?" the rebbe asked.

"What do you mean, Rebbe?" the man said sharply, making no attempt to hide his displeasure at having to make this detour. "I am earn-ing my living, running after my livelihood. There are opportunities for success ahead of me, and if I don't race after them they will escape me."

"And how do you know," the rebbe asked, "that these opportunities lie before you? Perhaps you are racing right by them? Or even worse, perhaps they are behind you and you are running away from them?"

The man simply stared at the rebbe uncomprehendingly.

"Listen, my friend." Reb Levi Yitzchak said, "I am not saying you should not earn a living. I am only worried that in your obsession with earning you are missing out on the living."

1 *Moshe Rabbeinu:* Literally, "Moses our Teacher." The Bible does not refer to Moses in this way. This is the title given to Moses by the Rabbis as a means of identifying him and his role with that of the Rabbis.

2 Sparks of God: The kabbalist Isaac Luria (1534–1572) taught that all things contain a spark of the Divine, and that the deepest spiritual work is to release those sparks and return them to God by using the things of this world in a righteous and honorable manner.

ℯ The way of Hasidism is never at the expense of this world. Your task is not to escape from this world but to hallow it. How? By engaging everything with the utmost respect and concern, and by not ignoring the physical even in the midst of the spiritual.

Reb Yaakov Shimshon's teaching here is quite radical. Moses is the fully realized spiritual leader of the Israelite people. Can it be that even he was misdirected in his union with God? Can it be that mere bread and water can take precedent over communing with the source and substance of all reality? Yes! Even Moses—or perhaps especially Moses—needed to focus on the ordinary. The more spiritual you are, the more careful you must be not to separate yourself from the material.

God first appears to Moses in a burning bush (Exodus 3:1–10). Commentators have made much of the lowly character of the bush. It is nothing special. God manifests through the ordinary. When you see God in the ordinary, it may for the moment appear extraordinary, but it is the ordinariness of things that really matters.

For this reason, the Rabbis took great care in their dealings with everyday things. Honoring matter was a way of honoring God. Some believe that the material is opposed to the spiritual, but this is not true. Material is the way in which the spirit manifests in the world of the five senses. When you honor the material, you honor the spiritual.

☐ The Loaf's Complaint

Reb Yaakov Shimshon of Kosov loved to share with his students the stories of the great rebbes and their Hasidim. It once happened after morning prayer that the rebbe began to tell one story after another without stopping. He and his Hasidim were lifted to such a state of divine rapture that they stepped out of time. The day passed, and it wasn't until late in the afternoon that the rebbe told his final tale.

Slowly, Reb Yaakov and his disciples returned to the needs of the everyday world and realized that they had eaten neither breakfast nor lunch. One of the students stood up and honored his rebbe, saying: "Until this moment, Rebbe, I did not really understand *Moshe Rabbeinu*[1] when he said that while on Mount Sinai he ate no bread and drank no water. Now I know what it is like to be filled with the very Presence of God and to feel no further need to eat or drink."

Reb Yaakov nodded his appreciation to his student and said, "Your interpretation is a worthy one, my son, but perhaps Moshe was not celebrating his transcendence of food and drink, but regretting it? We know that everything in this world contains a spark of the Divine and that only when a thing is used properly is this spark uplifted and repaired to God, from Whom it came.[2] This is no less true of food and drink than it is of books and tools. Moshe realized that in those forty days on Mount Sinai he neither ate nor drank and thus failed to uplift the divine sparks in his bread and water. In the World to Come, these sparks will complain to the Holy One that Moshe did them a grave disservice by putting his own love of God before their liberation."

1 *Ayn Keloheinu* (literally, "There is nothing like our God"): According to the ritual of the Hasidim, this prayer is recited daily as part of the concluding section of the Morning Prayer service.

2 Minyan (Hebrew for "number," plural *minyanim*): The quorum of ten adults needed for public worship. In Hasidic and Orthodox Jewish communities, only men qualify for a minyan; outside of these communities, women have achieved full equality in the service.

3 *Batlan:* Yiddish for "a good-for-nothing."

@ "Compare and contrast" is not only a classic high school essay assignment but the very essence of what you are all about. Your sense of self depends on comparing and contrasting. But what happens when you are dealing with something that has no other with which to be compared?

This is the problem you face when you try to imagine God. God cannot be separated from the rest of reality, so no comparing and contrasting is possible. Trying to know God in this way is like trying to bite your own teeth or smell your own nose. It just can't be done.

Knowing God becomes the ultimate *koan:* the ultimate mind-game that leads to awakening. If you persist with the puzzle, your ego-self dissolves, and there is a knowing that has nothing to do with you as the knower. This is what Reb Yaakov Yitzchak discovered every time he tried to imagine what God is like. His mind collapsed, and he fainted. That is, his sense of separate self dissolved into the nonduality of God as the Source and substance of all reality. He was, as the *Maggid* said, a *batlan,* good for nothing: good for the No-thing that is God.

☐ Nothing but God

It was the custom of Rabbi Dov Ber, the *Maggid* of Mezritch, to pray alone each morning. When he came to the *Ayn Keloheinu*[1] prayer at the end of his devotions, however, he would ask one of his Hasidim to gather a minyan[2] so he could conclude his prayer in community.

One morning, the gathering minyan included a young man named Reb Yaakov Yitzchak Horowitz, who, years later, would become the *Chozeh* of Lublin. When the *Maggid* saw that Reb Yaakov Yitzchak was one of the ten called to pray with him, he complained: "Can we not find someone other than this *batlan*?[3] He will only cause us trouble!"

The *Maggid*'s students were stunned at the abrasive tone and insulting words of their rebbe, but no one spoke up. On the other hand, no one raced off to find a substitute for Reb Yaakov Yitzchak.

"So be it," the *Maggid* sighed. Returning to his prayer, he called aloud: "*Ayn Keloheinu*, there is none like our God!" He had barely completed this opening line of the prayer when Reb Yaakov Yitzchak fainted and fell to the floor.

As the *Maggid* and his students rushed to help their fallen colleague, Reb Dov Ber said: "I told you he was a *batlan* and would disturb our prayers. All I said was 'There is nothing like God,' and immediately he realized the inner meaning of the words: 'There is nothing but God.' Realizing this, his sense of separateness left him, and he fainted. If you had found someone else, he wouldn't have grasped the meaning, and we would be done with our prayers by now."

1 HaBaD: School of Hasidism founded by Shneur Zalman. HaBaD is an acronym for *Hokhmah*/Wisdom, *Binah*/Understanding, and *Da'at*/Knowledge, three aspects of the Divine Mind manifest in humans as intuition, reason, and awareness. HaBaD emphasized panentheism, seeing the world as a manifestation of God based on the teaching in Isaiah: "The whole earth is filled with God's glory" (Isaiah 6:5). The goal of HaBaD is *bittul ha-yesh*, the annihilation of the seemingly separate self, and hence all existence, as perceived by that self, into the absolute unity of God.

2 Alter Rebbe: Yiddish for "Old Rabbi." Reb Schneur Zalman of Liadi, (1745-1812), founder of HaBaD Hasidism.

3 *Tanya:* Written by Reb Schneur Zalman and published in 1814; the first systematic exposition of Hasidic teaching.

4 Psalm 22:28.

@ What is the difference between a Hasid and a rebbe, a disciple and a master? The Hasid becomes fixated on the sign; the master looks beyond it to that toward which it points. What is the work of the rebbe? If the Hasid is lost in ideas, the rebbe points to the concrete. If the Hasid is lost in the concrete, the rebbe points to ideas. The work of the rebbe is to free the Hasid from thinking that God is in one place or the other, and to help the Hasid discover that God is in all as all.

Reb Dov Ber is the Hasid lost in abstraction: What does it mean that the peoples of all nations shall bow down before God? Schneur Zalman is the rebbe waiting to counter the Hasid's fantasy with the ice-water shock of concrete reality.

The goal is not to be imaginative or literal, but both; allowing the mind to open to all and get stuck on none.

☐ Praying with the World

It is the custom of certain HaBaD[1] Hasidim to insert into their prayers moments of silent contemplation, when they focus their thoughts on Hasidic insights and teachings that illumine the deeper meanings of the prayer they are about to recite.

It once happened that the Alter Rebbe,[2] Reb Schneur Zalman of Liadi, author of the *Tanya*[3] and founder of HaBaD, asked his son, Reb Dov Ber of Lubavitch, to share with him the Hasidic texts he was currently using in his meditations.

"I have been contemplating the text that reads 'And the peoples of all nations shall prostrate themselves before You.'"[4]

Dov Ber then asked his father, "And with what do you pray?"

"With the bench and the floor," the Alter Rebbe said.

1 *D'veikus* (literally, "union with God"): Because the whole world is filled with divine glory (Isaiah 6:5), we are all and always one with God. What is achieved is not union per se, but *da'at d'veikus,* awareness of union. Union cannot be achieved; it is a given. What must be achieved is seeing through the illusion that union must be achieved.

2 *Hispashtus hagashimius:* Dropping the material form.

ℓ Which are you: a cable or a hair?

In the early years of spiritual practice, we are cables. We struggle with the discipline. We wrestle ourselves into submission. We seek to control our thoughts, words, and deeds and to conform to a fixed pattern set by our teachers and sages. In time we adapt, and things do get easier; but do not mistake this lessening of effort for being a hair.

One does not shift from cable to hair; one simply stops being a cable. We stop being cables when we realize that effort is not getting us anywhere. Slowly the truth dawns on us that there is no "where" to go to. God is always here and now. We are always in a state of union with God because God is everything. What is lacking is not union but awareness of union.

Awareness requires no work at all. When you have forgotten someone's name, or are working hard on a problem, you screw up your face to intensify your thinking. Your brow furrows, but your thoughts are not thereby enhanced. On the contrary, they are more thick and heavy than before. It is only when you relax and stop thinking about the problem that the solution often bubbles to the surface. You did not do anything to make this happen, you simply stopped doing those things that keep it from happening.

The cable never stops trying. The hair never starts.

☐ A Kiss Good-Bye

It is not uncommon among Hasidim to find people calling out loudly in the midst of their prayers. Yet, the custom of Reb Pinchas of Korets was just the opposite. When he prayed, his voice never rose above a whisper, and his body remained still and calm. Wishing to understand the way of their rebbe, several of Reb Pinchas' senior students inquired after his manner of prayer.

"What is the essence of prayer?" he asked them.

"*D'veikus*,"[1] they replied, "becoming one with the One."

"Yes," Reb Pinchas said, "and the essence of *d'veikus* is *hispashtus hagashmius*,[2] dropping awareness of the separate self, body and mind. This happens naturally when one dies. Our sages said that for some, death is like hauling a thick ship's cable from the dock to the ship through a narrow hole; it has to be yanked and pulled, and it flaps and flops around in the process. For others, death resembles a kiss and is as smooth and as soft as pulling a strand of hair from a glass of milk.

"The same is true in prayer. For some, the temporary death of the self in prayer is like hauling on board a thick cable. There is much grunting and groaning, and the body flails this way and that. For others, prayer is a kiss from God in which the body and mind simply slip away in silence and stillness. You, my friends, may be like cables. I am a simple hair."

1 *Davven Shacharit:* Literally, "pray the Morning Prayer service."

2 *Talmud:* The authoritative body of rabbinic law and legend spanning seven centuries from 200 B.C.E. to 500 C.E.

3 Rabbi Akiva (45–135): According to tradition, Rabbi Akiva was an illiterate shepherd whose wife, Rachel, encouraged him to leave home and study. He returned many years later with thousands of disciples. Hence Akiva's teaching: "Who is wealthy? A man with a virtuous wife" (*Shabbat* 25b). Akiva supported the Bar Kochba rebellion against the Roman occupation of Israel. He was arrested and tortured to death at the age of ninety.

@ When it comes to prayer and spiritual practice, you must walk at your own pace. The purpose of practice is not to get from "here" to "there" but to realize that "there" is always "here." Spiritual practice must be done *lishmah,* for its own sake, without a goal or purpose. You walk for the pleasure of walking; you sit for the pleasure of sitting; you pray for the pleasure of praying. When we turn practice into work, we mistake its true nature as play.

Conventional language regarding spirituality tends to focus on work-related words. We speak of spiritual practice, discipline, effort, work. In Hebrew we use the term *avodah,* work, to refer to prayer and meditation practices. These words distract us from the truth about spirituality. Work is all about earning something, doing something, getting somewhere. But spirituality is all about accepting, receiving, embracing, and surrendering. It is as if we want spirituality to be difficult so as to excuse our not bothering with it.

Better to speak of spiritual play than spiritual work. Play can be no less intense and engaging, but it doesn't hold out the hope of a prize. You play for the sheer fun of playing. When your spiritual life is done for joy, your life will be filled with joy.

☐ Praying with; Praying among

While traveling through a small town, Reb Uri of Strelisk stopped to *davven Shacharit*[1] with the local congregation. As was his practice, Reb Uri lengthened the prayers and entered into ecstatic revelry. After the service had ended, the rabbi of the town spoke to Reb Uri in private.

"Does it not occur to you, Rebbe, that your ecstasy and lengthening of the prayers is an inconvenience upon the congregation? After all, the Talmud[2] tells us that Rabbi Akiva[3] prayed with such intensity that he would begin his prayers in one corner of a room and end them in another. Because of this he chose to pray alone. On those occasions when he did pray with the congregation, he used to keep his prayers brief so as not to inconvenience anyone."

Reb Uri replied: "Perhaps there is another way to understand the Talmud's teaching on this matter. When our sages tell us that Rabbi Akiva prayed with the congregation, they mean to tell us that the congregation accompanied their rabbi on his ecstatic journey. Because they were all praying with such intensity, there was no need to lengthen the prayers. When our sages tell us that Rabbi Akiva prayed alone, they mean to say that he alone among the congregation was praying with the proper intensity, and in these cases he had to work much harder and longer to bring them along.

"This would be like you and I walking to the market. If we walked at the same swift pace, our walk would be short. But if you insisted on walking at half my pace, I would have to wait for you to catch up so that we are not each walking alone. This would mean making the walk much longer."

1 *Rebbitzin:* The wife of a rabbi.

2 *Shul* (literally, "school"): A Yiddish word used to describe a traditional Eastern European synagogue. The name can be traced to the Romans, who called the synagogue *schola* in deference to its educational function in the Jewish community.

3 *Gut in Himmel:* Yiddish for "God in heaven."

4 *Beis midrash:* House of study, often attached to a synagogue.

5 *Shabbos:* The Sabbath.

6 *Ribbono shel Olam,* Master of the Universe: A term of endearment applied to God.

7 *Ruach HaKodesh:* The Holy Spirit of God that manifests in people, leading to prophetic visions and teachings.

@ What you do for yourself alone is not the work of the Holy Spirit. What you do for others is. Spiritual work is surrendering yourself to the spirit of service. The means must be appropriate to the need, but the intent is always the same: helping another in need.

☐ Stick Angels

Rebbitzin[1] Mirl, wife of Reb Yitzchak Meir of Mezhibuzh and daughter-in-law of Reb Avraham Yehoshua Heschel of Apta, was praying in *shul*[2] when she heard a great commotion coming from the men's side of the synagogue. Inquiring into the matter, she learned that Reb Yaakov the wagon-driver had died.

"*Gut in Himmel,*"[3] the *rebbitzin* shouted. "Do any of you know what kind of man he was?"

When people had gathered close to the *rebbitzin* in order to hear, she said: "One winter when I had not even a stick of kindling for a fire, Reb Yaakov took his wagon into the forest and returned with bundles of wood, enough for me and for the *beis midrash,*[4] where we huddled together to study Torah.

"And that is not all. One Friday I found myself without a drop of water in my house. Reb Yaakov heard of this and brought me a barrel filled to the very brim with water. Not only was I able to cook for *Shabbos,*[5] but my neighbors all around also shared this water and could do the same."

Suddenly the *rebbitzin* stood up. Lifting her face and voice to heaven, she cried: "*Ribbono shel Olam!*[6] May it be Your will that the divine sparks in every stick of wood and every drop of water he brought me become angels calling to You on his behalf, that he might be welcomed into heaven with a chorus of praise!"

A few minutes later the *rebbitzin's* husband came into the *shul* and was told of her bold request on Reb Yaakov's behalf. "What a woman I have married," Reb Yitzchak Meir said. "The *Ruach HaKodesh*[7] certainly rests with her, for what she asked has already been done."

1 *Nu:* Yiddish expression for "So?"

@ To be a connoisseur of people is to see the true value of each person. Seeing the true value of a person does not mean that we overlook people's flaws. On the contrary, we have to find a way of honoring the person despite her or his flaws.

Where do our flaws come from? Are we born flawed? The Torah says that "the imagination of a person's heart is evil from his youth" (Genesis 8:21). This suggests that it is not we who are flawed, but our imaginations. Sometime in our early years, perhaps around six or so, we begin to imagine that we are separate, independent, and autonomous creatures in competition with other humans and perhaps life itself for our personal survival. We imagine ourselves to be an independent "I" and the rest of life to be "other." As our sense of alienation from the other grows, our ability to excuse our evil and exploitative behavior grows as well. And all of this comes from a flawed imagination.

Reb Shalom Ber was a connoisseur of people. He understood the flawed imagination and how it defines our world. Unlike Reb Monye, he did not equate flaws with rejects. In Reb Monye's business, flawed diamonds are discarded. In Reb Shalom Ber's business, flawed people are simply diamonds in the rough; they need cutting and polishing. We cut the rough human by pointing out the flawed imagination and the anxious and painful world it creates. We polish the rough human by treating her with justice and compassion, and responding not to her flawed imagination but to the pure divine diamond that is obscured by the imagination.

When you meet another, do you see the flaws or the gem? Do you respond from imagination or from truth?

☐ The Connoisseur

Reb Monye Monissohn, a wealthy diamond merchant, went to visit his rebbe, Reb Shalom Ber of Lubavitch. Reb Monye was eager to show the rebbe some of the diamonds he had recently purchased in the hope of getting a blessing for the success of his business. The rebbe seemed more interested in extolling the praises of certain common laborers whom Reb Monye had criticized for their lack of learning.

"Rebbe," the merchant said at last, "I just do not see what you see in these people. They are illiterate boors."

"In fact, Reb Monye," the rebbe replied, "each of them has many honorable traits."

"Maybe so, Rebbe, but I for one cannot see them."

The rebbe sat silently for a few moments. "Nu,[1] Reb Monye, show me your new diamonds."

Reb Monye eagerly untied a velvet sack and spread a glittering pool of diamonds on the rebbe's desk. Lifting one in particular to the light streaming in from a window, he said: "This one is especially fine, Rebbe."

"I see nothing special in it," Reb Shalom Ber said.

"I would not expect you to, Rebbe. One must be a connoisseur of gems to see what makes each one worthy of such praise."

"Every person is also a gem, my dear Reb Monye," the rebbe said. "And just as with your diamonds, you must be a connoisseur to see them truly."

1 Shofar: Ram's horn. Since the destruction of the Second Temple in 70 C.E., the shofar has been associated primarily with Rosh Hashanah, the Jewish New Year. The Order of the Blowing of the Shofar is a set ritual of one hundred notes, broken up into three categories: *teki'ah,* a continuous rising note; *teru'ah,* nine short notes; and *shevarim,* three wailing notes.

2 Rosh Hashanah: The Jewish New Year, the first of ten consecutive Days of Awe, when Jews engage in self-reflection and forgiveness.

3/4 *Kavvanot:* (Hebrew for "intention," singular *kavvanah*): Mystical focal points associated with different ritual acts. By attending to the *kavvanah* associated with the action about to be undertaken, the doer uplifts the doing to an act of spiritual healing.

5 *Davvenen:* Worship.

6 *Yesher koach:* (literally, "straight power"): A common Hebrew phrase of encouragement and praise equal to "Right on!" in colloquial English.

@ What is this ax that brooks no lock? The broken heart. When you realize that you cannot cultivate all the keys needed, when you realize that all your spiritual effort is a subtle support of the ego, when you realize that there is nothing you can do to enter the room of awakening, your heart breaks, and with it all the doors and their locks shatter as well.

☐ Bursting the Gates

The Baal Shem Tov asked Reb Wolff Kitzis, one of his senior disciples, to blow the shofar[1] for Rosh Hashanah.[2] To help focus his mind during the blowing, the Baal Shem Tov suggested that Reb Wolff study the kabbalistic *kavvanot*[3] assigned to the shofar. Reb Wolff devoted himself diligently to the study and wrote notes to take with him to review before blowing the shofar to ensure that his mind would be directed properly.

When it came time for Reb Wolff to go to shul for the holy day and blow the shofar, he looked for his notes, but in vain. And what was worse: without his notes his mind too went blank. Not a single *kavvanah*[4] could he recall. And so it was that when Reb Wolff stepped before the congregation to blow the shofar he did so with an empty mind and a broken heart.

After the *davvenen*[5] came to a close, the Baal Shem Tov turned to Reb Wolff and cried: "*Yesher koach!*[6] Never have I heard such a powerful shofar blowing!"

"But Master," Reb Wolff said, "I forgot every word I studied and blew the shofar with no *kavvanah* except the sheer humility of one who knows nothing!"

The Baal Shem Tov smiled and said: "My dear Reb Wolff. In the palaces of earthly kings there are many rooms, each with its own particular key. But one with an ax can enter them all. If this is true of earthly kings, all the more so is it true of the King of Kings. The *kavvanot* are the keys to each room, but one whose heart is humble can burst into any room!"

1 Deuteronomy 4:30.

2 In this context, the Hebrew word *ad* means either "unto" or "until."

3 *Adonai Elohecha:* A common phrase in the Hebrew Bible, thought to unite what was once two different ideas of God: *Adonai,* the euphemism for the unpronounceable YHVH referring to the unknowable and transcendent God, and *Elohim,* the immanent God present to us in and through nature.

4 *Elohim* (plural Hebrew noun used for singular God): The Jewish mystical understanding of why *Elohim* is a plural noun linked with singular verbs is that the Torah is trying to teach us that the One God is manifest in, and is the plurality of, creation.

@ *Teshuvah* is a process of stripping away selfishness by recognizing and repenting the mistakes the self makes.

Think of your soul as a clear pane of glass transparent to the Light of God. The glass itself is pure, hence the daily Jewish affirmation: *Elohai nishamah sheh natata-be t'horah he,* "My God, the soul You breathe into me is pure." Yet, the ego often smears the glass with selfish acts that distort or block out the Light. These acts of selfishness must be cleansed so that the glass can do what it is created to do: allow the Light to pass through it. *Teshuvah* is the act of cleansing the glass.

How long do you need to do this? Forever. Even when the transcendent and immanent are one and the same to you, even when you realize that both self and selfishness are part of God, you must still cleanse the glass. At this point, your cleansing is filled with compassion for the self, and you clean without self-condemnation. But you still clean.

☐ Perfect Repentance

The *Maggid* of Mezritch was expounding on the Torah verse "You shall make *teshuvah ad Adonai Elohecha;* You shall repent until the Lord your God."**1**

"What is the meaning of this strange phrasing?" the *Maggid* asked. "Should Torah not say 'You shall repent <u>unto</u> *Adonai Elohecha,* the Lord your God' rather than <u>until</u>?**2** And why say both *Adonai* and *Elohecha* when either one would suffice?"**3**

Answering his own question, the *Maggid* said, "To understand the first, you must understand the second. What is the meaning of *Adonai?*"

A Hasid replied: "*Adonai* is the four-letter Name of God that signifies the absolute transcendence of the Divine."

"And what is the meaning of *Elohecha?*"

"This refers to *Elohim,***4** the Name of God that signifies the absolute immanence of God."

"And what is the meaning of *teshuvah?*"

"*Teshuvah* is the process of returning to God by admitting our mistakes and making amends."

"So," the *Maggid* said, "We are to continue the process of *teshuvah* until we can see *Adonai* manifest as *Elohim,* <u>until</u> we see the one and the many as different aspects of the One and Only."

@ The Hasidim teach that there are five kinds of people in the world: the Perfectly Evil Person, who acts without remorse; the Imperfectly Evil Person, who acts with remorse; the Perfectly Good Person, who acts without any sense of self or selfishness; the Imperfectly Good Person, who acts with some sense of self and selfishness; and the *Beinoni*, the Inbetweener, who experiences life as a battle between selfishness and selflessness.

The Perfectly Evil and Good persons receive no punishment or reward for their actions, for they are incapable of doing other than they do. The Imperfectly Evil and Good persons can experience consequences for their actions, for they know that what they do is either evil or good, but this knowing is so fleeting as to be almost imperceptible. It is the Inbetweener that truly wrestles with good and evil.

For this wrestling to be real, the capacity to sin must also be real. Evil is not an illusion but a force from God that needs direction. Evil is not to be eradicated but channeled toward the good. Only the Inbetweener can do this, for only the Inbetweener knows good and evil as real forces in her life.

Rabbi Levi Yitzchak is revealing a great truth to this violent thief: It is because of his intimate knowledge of evil that he is capable of turning toward the good. His sins need not be a stumbling block to redemption, but a catalyst for it.

The same is true of you. Do not think that your misdeeds prevent you from choosing good over evil. You can turn to God at any time, and when you do, your evil deeds will be seen as guideposts leading you to redemption, not fenceposts keeping you from it.

☐ The Value of Sin

Reb Levi Yitzchak of Berditchev was once accosted by a highway robber known for his violence and acts of depravity. The thief grabbed Levi Yitzchak by his coat and dragged the rebbe from his coach. Pushing him up against the coach door, the man shouted, "Do you know who I am?"

"Yes," the rebbe said calmly, "and I must admit to being envious of you as well."

"You dare to jest at my expense?" the man screamed, his lips almost touching Reb Levi Yitzchak's nose. "What do you mean—you envy me? What is there about me, a dangerous felon, that you, a sainted rabbi, should envy?"

"Our sages teach," the rebbe said, "that God so loves the sinner that one who repents of his sins out of love of God has all of his wickedness counted as deeds of merit. Now take myself: My sins are few and minor, and whatever good God credits me with is not helped by these transgressions. But you! You are famous for wicked deeds. If you were to repent out of love for God, no one could match you in merit! And for this I envy you!"

That said, Reb Levi Yitzchak grabbed the robber by his lapels and begged him so compassionately to repent that the thief's heart melted, and he returned to God right then and there.

1 *Esrog* (Hebrew for citron): One of the four species of plant (along with palm, willow, and myrtle) that is used in the harvest festival of Sukkos (Leviticus 23:40). These four plants are held together and waved in the six directions (north, south, east, west, up, and down) to thank God for the bounty of nature that surrounds us.

2 Sukkos (Hebrew for "booths"; singular, *sukkah*): One of the three pilgrimage holy days mentioned in the Hebrew Bible (the other two are Passover and Shavuos). Agriculturally, Sukkos is a harvest festival celebrating the earth's bounty and looking forward to good rains for the next harvest. The main observances of Sukkos are the waving of the four species (see above) and living in temporary huts called *sukkos*. These huts are reminiscent of the temporary shelters in which the Israelites dwelt during their forty years of desert wandering, and are constructed in honor of those Israelites in Sinai.

ℯ "I have set before you life and death, blessing and curse; therefore choose life that you and your descendents may live" (Deuteronomy 30:19).

Making choices for life is at the heart of all spiritual discipline. It may be the most important discipline of all, for it forces you to face the choices, determine which is for life, and then act accordingly. Facing the choices means slowing down enough to notice them. Determining which is for life requires you to have cultivated the presence of mind and clarity of insight needed to distinguish between the desires of the self and the needs of others. Acting accordingly necessitates cultivating nonattachment so that you can save all year for an *esrog* and yet use those savings to buy a horse for a stranger. Choosing life isn't an alternative to other spiritual practices; it is the culmination of the practice in the ordinary moments of your everyday life.

☐ A Four-Legged Esrog

In addition to being rabbi of his community, Reb Mordechai of Neshchiz was a prudent businessman. After every business trip he would set aside money from his profits to help the poor. He would also set aside a small sum in order to have enough to buy a fine esrog[1] for Sukkos.[2] As the holy day drew near, Reb Mordechai collected his esrog money and set off to Brody to purchase the fruit.

When he arrived at the edge of the city, he came across the town's water carrier, sobbing on the side of the road. Reb Mordechai stopped and asked the man what troubled him.

"Do you see my wagon over there? It is a fine strong wagon. When it is filled with barrels of water and harnessed to a strong and loyal horse, I can do a fine day's work feeding not only myself and my family, but the poor as well."

"So what is the trouble?"

"The barrels I have," said the man. "The water I know where to get. And the wagon, well, there it is."

"And the horse," Reb Mordechai said softly.

"Yes, the horse. My horse is dead. Died this morning, and with her my livelihood as well."

"Wait here," the rebbe said. "Let me see what I can do." Walking into town, Reb Mordechai found a horse trader and bought a strong young horse with his esrog money. He returned to the man and presented him with this fine horse. "I came to Brody to buy an esrog; instead, I have purchased a horse. But it is all the same, for God commands us to buy an esrog, and God commands us to help others in need. So, my friends, they shall say their blessing over a fruit; I shall say mine over a horse."

1 *Rebbitzin:* The wife of a rabbi.

ℯ We are all lame—if not in body, then in mind. We are hobbled by crippling ideas. You are the ideas you hold, the stories you tell about yourself, your upbringing, your dreams and goals. And these ideas and stories are often inherited; they are not original to you, but simply things you have heard so often and at vulnerable times in your life that they have become a part of you. It is as if you become so ardently attached to a role that you forget you are an actor playing that role.

Who would you be without these precious ideas and stories? Imagine a person who suffers from severe amnesia. Her story is gone, along with her memory. Often the person that remains isn't at all the same person that was there before the amnesia set in. Now imagine that you have amnesia. You can no longer remember the childhood traumas, adolescent angst, and adult struggles that excuse your moral lapses and explain your everyday dis-ease. You are no longer driven by habit, because you no longer remember that to which you are habituated. Who are you without all the remembered conditioning of the past?

When Reb Chaim the lame forgot to be Reb Chaim the lame and became simply an ecstatic lover of God, he forgot the limitations of his crippled leg. If you are ever going to remember who you really are—God manifest here and now—you must first forget who you think you are.

☐ The Better Leg

Reb Chaim of Zanz was lame. His right leg was of almost no use to him. Yet, when he prayed he did so with such fervor that he would leap up on his right leg and dance, totally absorbed in union with God.

One day he visited the community of Reb Naftali of Ropshitz, and there he cleaved so tightly to God that he hopped and danced and spun on his bad leg over and over again. The *rebbitzin*[1] happened by and saw what was happening. Complaining to her husband, she said: "Why do you let him dance like that on his bad leg? Tell him to dance on his good leg."

Reb Naftali said: "My sweet wife, if Reb Chaim knew on which leg he was dancing, I promise you I would speak to him as you have suggested. But what am I to do if in his passionate love of God he no longer remembers he is lame?"

@ How might these principles play out in your life?

Do not spoil anything new. Many of us spoil the new simply by insisting that it conform to the old. The past is a shield against the future. Life lived in such a manner is imitative. There is no creativity, only conformity. The new is not allowed to be new and must masquerade as the old.

Fix anything old. The old needs fixing when it no longer functions in the way it was intended. This principle is especially important in the world of conventional religion. It is the nature of religion to fixate on form and forget the principle the form originally embodied. The result is a hollow imitation of deeds without the ethics and joy the deeds once cultivated. How do we fix this? Not by abandoning the deeds but by returning to the principle behind them and reinventing the deed to better embody the idea. Where are you spoiling the new by insisting that it conform to the old? Where are you conforming to the old simply because it is old, and no longer living the principle behind the deed?

☐ Two Rules

At the wedding of the son of Reb Avraham Yaakov of Sadigora to the daughter of Reb Zvi HaKohen of Rimanov, the groom's grandfather, Reb Yisrael of Ruzhin, stood up and said to the father of the bride: "Let me share with you the *yichus* of our family. My great-grandfather was Reb Dov Ber; my grandfather was his son, Reb Avraham, who was called the Angel; my great-uncle was Reb Nachum of Chernobyl; and my uncle was his son, Reb Mordechai of Chernobyl. So, my dear friend, please share with us your lineage."

"My parents died when I was ten years of age," Reb Zvi said softly. "I did not know them well enough to tell you anything about them other than that they were righteous and good-hearted people. After their deaths, a relative apprenticed me to a tailor, for whom I worked for five years. It was during that time that I learned two rules by which I have governed my life: *Do not spoil anything new*, and *fix anything old*."

With that, the groom's grandfather leaped to his feet, shouting joyously: "This is a marriage of two great lineages. These children are doubly blessed!"

1 *Tish:* A meal shared by a rebbe and his Hasidim.

2 *L'Chayyim* (Hebrew, "To Life!"): A traditional toast.

3 *Birkat HaMazon* (Grace after Meals): A series of prayers recited after any meal at which bread is eaten. The idea of saying grace after meals comes from the Torah: "When you have eaten and are satisfied, you shall bless the Lord your God for the good land which God has given you" (Deuteronomy 8:10).

@ Reb Menachem Mendel taught through silence. What, then, did Reb Beirish hear? He heard the sound of the *Shekhinah,* the Holy Presence, manifest in and through himself. Had the rebbe taught through speech, Reb Beirish would have heard the rebbe's words, compared them with those he had heard from other rebbes at other times, and filed them away in his memory to be trotted out if needed some time in the future. But through the rebbe's silence, Reb Beirish could hear what he had never heard before: the ever-present revelation of God.

Revelation is immediate and momentary, continuous rather than continual. It comes through intuition rather than logic; it is right-brained rather than left. To hear it, you must be silent. But being silent is not the same as being passive. You have to offer all you know to the silence and allow it to be torn down. What is torn down is what you know; what is built up is what you didn't know. But the new becomes the old, and so the sacrifice must be made again and again.

Rest on nothing, and your foundation is secure.

☐ A Powerful Silence

At the *tish*[1] of most rebbes, hours pass in heated Torah discussion, punctuated by much dancing and drinking *L'chayyim*.[2] But at the table of Reb Menachem Mendel of Vorki, very little was said, for the rebbe's way was the way of silence.

At one particular *tish*, Reb Beirish of Biala was in attendance. Expecting the verbal exchange common to most rebbes, Reb Beirish was soon caught up in the deep silence of this quiet sage. Hours passed, and not a word was spoken. Even the breathing of those assembled fell into silence, and only the buzzing of an occasional fly broke the silence.

After they had finished eating, the rebbe led the community in *Birkat HaMazon*,[3] and then they all left for their respective homes. Worried that their honored guest was annoyed at the quality of their rebbe's *tish*, several Hasidim approached and asked Reb Beirish how he was faring.

Reb Beirish said: "What a *tish* the rebbe gave! He taught me lessons in Torah I have heard nowhere else! And every one of his challenges tore down my understanding of Torah and rebuilt it from the ground up. But I didn't take his challenge passively. I answered every question he asked of me!"

The Hasidim smiled and welcomed Reb Beirish as one of them.

@ Are you asleep or awake? And more important: Do you know the damage you do in either state?

There are three types of people: the sleeping, the waking, and the awakened. The sleeping see God as separate from the world: the One separate from the many. There is God and there is creation: two separate realities. The waking see the One at the cost of the many: God is real, but creation is illusory. They revel in the glory of the forest, never noticing the uniqueness of each tree. The awakened see the One as the many. To them, God is both the source of life and the substance that is living. Here the distinction between God and creation is quantitative rather than qualitative. Each tree is a part of the forest, but no tree is the forest itself.

Reb Shalom Ber warns us that asleep or awake, we can do damage. What is the damage of the sleeper? To exploit the other in the name of the One. What is the damage of the waking person? To demand conformity as the proper response to unity. What is the damage of the awakened? To allow the damage of the other two to continue without resistance.

Reb Shalom Ber challenges his son to awaken fully from the nightmare of duality without being trapped in the false surety of monism. He urges him to see the forest and the trees, to know that the One and the many are both manifestations of the nondual God.

☐ The Leaf

Reb Shalom Ber of Lubavitch once took his family to a summer resort in the country. Going for a walk with his son and eventual successor, Reb Yosef Yitzchak, Reb Shalom pointed to the ears of corn covering the surrounding farmland.

"Behold divinity!" the rebbe said. "Each stalk of corn, and every movement it makes, is a manifestation of the mind of God. Creation is the thought of God expressed as the physicality of the world."

Reb Yosef Yitzchak listened to his father's words and soon found himself lost in the wondrous realization that this world, his body, and all bodies were expressions of God. As he walked, he brushed against a tree and plucked a leaf from its stem. Absentmindedly tearing the leaf into strips, he slipped deeper and deeper into joyous contemplation.

"Yosef Yitzchak!" the rebbe called to him sternly, breaking his son's concentration and returning him to the world of their walk. "We are speaking of God manifest in creation, and here you rip a leaf from its place and destroy it for no reason at all. Do you imagine that this leaf has no purpose in this world but to sacrifice itself to your thoughtlessness? Is its 'I' of lesser value than your own? You are different, yes, but superior? No. Everything has its divinely directed purpose, and you have made it impossible for this leaf to achieve its reason for being."

Reb Yosef Yitzchak was ashamed of his behavior. His father said: "Remorse is good. Now learn from it. For our sages say, 'A person can do damage whether awake or asleep.'"

1 | *Beis midrash* (literally, "House of Study"): The school.

℮ | Sometimes you must sacrifice one piece to gain two. What is the one whose death brings you two? The inflated ego. If you desire the love of another, then sacrifice the love of self, put the other first, and you will discover that in feeding another you, too, are filled.

You may move only one space at a time. You cannot rush life. Long or short, troubled or joyous, life unfolds one moment at a time. Ecclesiastes teaches "there is a time for every purpose under heaven" (Ecclesiastes 3:1). Do not cry when it is time to laugh or gather stones at a time for scattering. Know what time it is, and allow it to run its course.

You may only move forward. The past is finished. You cannot undo what has been done. There are no rehearsals and no "do overs." You can learn from the past, but you cannot remake it. You can replay it over and over, but it always turns out the same, and in the meantime you are missing out on the only time there is: now.

When you reach the top, you are free to move anywhere you wish. But there is nowhere to go! Birthing, dying, loving, hating, embracing, fleeing—it is all here. Top and bottom, here and there, past and future—all gone. You win! And then, realizing the fun is in playing the game, you, like Reb Nachum, set up the board for another round. Playing is its own reward.

□ Rules of the Game

Reb Nachum of Stefansti surprised his Hasidim in the *beis midrash*[1] one night during Hanukkah. Instead of finding his students deep in the study of Torah, he found them equally engrossed in a game of Chinese checkers.

Embarrassed at their game, the Hasidim made to put the pieces away, when the rebbe smiled and had them set up for a new match.

"Do you know the rules of this game?" he asked them. No one said a word.

"Good," the rebbe said. "Then I will share them with you. First, you sometimes have to sacrifice one piece in order to gain two. Second, you may never move two spaces at once. Third, you may only move forward and never backward. And fourth, when you've reached the top, you may move anywhere you like!"

Looking from one face to the other, he added: "And the rules of this game are the rules of our game as well."

1 HaBaD: The school of Hasidism founded by Reb Shneur Zalman. HaBaD is an acronym for *Hokhmah, Binah, Da'at,* three aspects of the Divine Mind experienced by humans as intuition, reason, and awareness.

2 *Yechidus* (from the Hebrew *yachad,* unity): A private interview between Hasid and rebbe wherein the latter explores the former's soul to help direct the Hasid toward enlightenment.

3 *M'rirut* (bitterness): A contrite and humble state of mind that arises when one takes stock of one's thoughts, words, and deeds and realizes how far they are from the ideal. This feeling is a catalyst for improving the quality of one's life as expressed through thoughts, words, and deeds.

℮ Reb Yitzchak Aizik studied the externals, but the rebbe wants to encounter the heart. What good is knowing lots of ideas, or mastering complex and esoteric practices, when you are still ignorant of yourself? At the heart of spiritual awakening is the discovery that the self that is struggling to awaken is in fact that which is blocking the awakening. All this so-called spiritual mastery allows the ego to grow into megalomania, mistaking itself for God. The real work is to observe the slippery oil of ego and experience the bitterness at its root: the fear, anxiety, greed, ignorance, and anger that define it. The more you see the ego for what it is, the weaker the ego becomes. At last, all that remains is the perfume: just enough of a sense of self to function well in the world, but not enough to hamper your seeing God in, as, and through the world. Now you are ready to see the rebbe.

☐ Time to Visit

It was the custom of the Hasidim of Reb Shnuer Zalman of Liadi for newer students to postpone their first private visit with the rebbe until after they had studied the basic philosophy and practices of HaBaD[1] Hasidism with the rebbe's senior students. In this way, they hoped to use the time they would have with the rebbe to deal with deeper things.

In following this custom, Reb Yitzchak Aizik of Homil spent two and a half years preparing for this first *yechidus*.[2] On his way to visit his rebbe, he passed through the town of Kazan, near Polotzk. Seeing as this was the home of one of his rebbe's senior students, Reb Shaul, he thought it both wise and correct to drop in on the rabbi and pay his respects.

Learning that Reb Yitzchak Aizik was on his way to visit the rebbe, Reb Shaul said, "I once heard this from the very first Hasidim. It seems that when our rebbe created the HaBaD way of divine practice, he announced, 'Six months shall one spend with oils of myrrh, and six months with perfumes, before coming to me for *yechidus*.'"

Seeing that the meaning of this was lost on Reb Yitzchak Aizik, he said, "The oils of myrrh refer to meditations that give rise to *m'rirut*,[3] the bitterness caused by seeing deeply into all one's flaws and selfishness. The perfume is what is left after the oil has gone. What is left? A deep sensitivity to God manifest in the world around you. All this should be done before one goes to the rebbe for *yechidus*."

Hearing this, Reb Yitzchak thanked Reb Shaul and returned home for another twelve months of preparation.

1 *Pesach* (Passover): One of the three pilgrimage festivals mentioned in the Torah; like the other two, Sukkos and Shavuos, it has a historical, agricultural, and mystical dimension. Historically, *Pesach* marks the liberation of the Hebrews from Egyptian slavery; agriculturally, it celebrates the beginning of the barley harvest; kabbalistically, it is a period of deep introspection when we seek to free ourselves from the things that enslave us to the narrow places of selfishness and ego.

The kabbalists derive their understanding from a play on the Hebrew word for Egypt: *mitzrayim*. The Hebrew can be read as "Egypt" or as "from narrow places" (*mi* = from; *tzar* = narrow place; *im* = plural suffix). Egypt is, spiritually speaking, the narrow place of enslavement, and this can refer to any habit of heart, mind, or body that promotes selfishness and egotism.

2 *Bat Kol* (literally, "Daughter of a Voice," or "Echo"): An audible heavenly revelation.

@ What do you want from spiritual practice? Enlightenment? Bliss? Happiness? Salvation? An end to suffering? A place in paradise? As long as you have a reward in mind, your practice is tainted. Yet, is it possible to act with no goal in mind? Can the ego act without expecting something in return?

When one acts without a goal, with no sense of reward, the act itself becomes the point, and the reward is immediate. This is what all the great mystics know: The doing is the receiving! The doing is the salvation!

☐ Selfless Service

Once the Baal Shem Tov set out to journey to the Land of Israel. *Pesach*[1] was approaching, and he had no money with which to buy the needed supplies. A wealthy merchant, hearing of his plight, came forward and donated a generous amount of money that allowed the Baal Shem Tov to observe the holy week without worry. Knowing the man to be childless, the Baal Shem Tov blessed him for his generosity and promised him that within the year his wife would bear a child.

When the merchant had gone, a *Bat Kol*[2] pealed out from heaven: "Did you not know that this man's wife was barren? Because of your promise, the Holy One has to change the very course of nature. For this you will forfeit your place in the World to Come."

Rather than collapse in despair at having lost his heavenly reward, the Baal Shem Tov danced with joy. "Thank You," he called to God. "Before this I always worried that my service to You was tainted by the thought of reward, but now I have the opportunity to serve You with no thought of reward, for even the World to Come is closed to me!"

1 Shavuos (Hebrew, "weeks"): The second of three pilgrimage festivals. The name "weeks" comes from the Torah's instruction to count seven weeks between the Passover barley harvest and the second harvest fifty days later. Historically, Shavuos is said to be the anniversary of the revelation of the Ten Commandments on Mount Sinai. The mystics prepared for Shavuos with a special ritual called *Tikkun Lel Shavuos* (Repairing on the Eve of Shavuos). This was an all-night recitation of sacred texts intended to place the kabbalist in the receptive mindset to personally experience the revelation at dawn.

2 The Ten Commandments (*Aseret HaDibrot,* the Ten Sayings): The Commandments revealed by God at Mount Sinai seven weeks after the Hebrews' exodus from Egypt. The Ten Commandments are mentioned twice in the Torah: first in Exodus 20:1–14 and again in a slightly different version in Deuteronomy 5: 6–18. Moses ordered twice-daily recitation of the Ten Commandments (Deuteronomy 6: 6–7), and Jews used to recite them morning and evening. The Rabbis replaced this with the twice-daily recitation of the *Sh'ma* (Hear O Israel, the Lord our God, the Lord is One) when sectarians argued that only the Ten Commandments were revealed by God and hence took precedence over the other laws of Torah.

@ What is it you steal from yourself? The things you want most. And how do you rob yourself of these things? By trying too hard to get them. For example, you desire certainty, and to get it you study hard to know what is true. Yet, the more you study, the more you know you will never know enough to be certain of anything, and this anxiety robs you of the very thing you desire.

What you want is not to be taken, but to be received. Do not imagine that you must climb to the top of the mountain to grasp what you seek. On the contrary, you must stand at the bottom of the mountain and receive it as it rolls down of its own accord. The "winner" in life is not the one who reaches the highest peak but the one who knows how to wait at the lowest depths.

☐ Robbing Yourself

Reb Yechiel Meir of Gostynin went to study with Reb Menachem Mendel of Kotsk during the holy week of Shavuos.[1] Upon his return, his father-in-law asked, "What did you study during your time in Kotsk?"

"As it was Shavuos," Reb Yechiel Meir said, "we studied the Ten Commandments."[2]

"Amazing," his father-in-law teased. "Since it was also Shavuos here at home, we also studied the Ten Commandments. Do they receive the Commandments differently in Kotsk? And is that why you would journey so far to study what we study at home?"

"Yes, indeed!" Reb Yechiel Meir replied. "The Commandments are different in Kotsk."

"And how is that?" his father-in-law asked.

"What did you learn from the Commandment 'You shall not steal'?"

"We learned just what it says: You shall not take from another that which does not belong to you," replied his father-in-law.

"And therein lies the difference," Reb Yechiel Meir said. "Here you learned that 'You shall not steal' means you shall not steal from another. In Kotsk we learned that you shall not steal from yourself as well."

1 Deuteronomy 31:30.

ℯ What is the essential spiritual practice? Listening. God is forever whispering truth into your ears, and all you have to do is listen. It sounds so very easy, and it is; but its very simplicity is what keeps it hidden from us. Listening requires no mastery of postures or doctrine. It doesn't require us to affiliate with any group. It can be done alone and in community. It needs no special instruction or master instructor. One just listens.

What listening does require, however, is silence. You cannot hear another if you are constantly chattering yourself. You cannot hear God if you are forever distracted by the talk of self.

We avoid silence, though. It is too uncomfortable. Why? Because we suspect that what we hear will not be to the ego's liking. And it won't. So the ego erects complex structures of words to blot out God's teaching. Religion is often just such a structure. Using sacred words, chants, teachings, and the like, religion mesmerizes us with God-talk when it should be inviting us into God-listening.

If you want to hear God, listen.

☐ Until Our Completion

Reb Simcha Bunem of Pshischah once entered into the study of his rebbe, Reb Yaakov Yitzchak, the Yid HaKodesh of Pshischah. Before he could say a word Reb Yaakov Yitzchak said to him, "Cite some verse of Torah, and I will reveal its meaning to you."

Without a moment's hesitation, Simcha Bunem said: "And Moshe spoke in the ears of all the people of Israel the words of this poem, until their completion (*ad tumam*)."[1]

Instantly the rebbe shouted, "*Ad tumam*, until their completion!"

Reb Simcha Bunem was overjoyed with this interpretation of his rebbe and shared it with a friend, Reb Chanoch Henich of Alexander.

"But all the rebbe did was repeat the final two words of the text," Reb Chanoch complained. "This is nothing. What did you hear in this that brings you such joy?"

Simcha Bunem chided his friend, saying, "You are no ignoramus! Figure it out!"

"All right," Reb Chanoch frowned. "Let's see. 'And Moshe spoke in the ears of all the people of Israel the words of this poem, until their completion.' The key is in the grammar. If Moshe had been referring to the completion of the poem, he would have said, 'until its completion.' Because he spoke in the plural, he wasn't referring to the poem at all but to the people themselves. Hmmm. Ah! Until their completion! Until our completion! Until our perfection! The words of the poem remind us that our covenant with God will be repeated and repeated in each of our ears until it transforms each of our hearts. We are never abandoned; God never despairs of us and will teach us continually until we perfectly live the godliness we are called to embody!"

"That's it!" cried Simcha Bunem, and the two men danced in joy.

@ As the ancient Taoist sage Chuang Tzu might have said: "Are you a turkey pretending to be a human, or a human pretending to be a turkey?" There is no way to know for sure. You are what you think. So, if you do not like who you are, simply think otherwise.

Would that it were so easy. While you have the capacity to influence your thoughts, you do not have the capacity to control them. Thoughts happen faster than the ego that pretends to think them.

Do you actually think your thoughts, or do you simply become aware of them once they are thought? If you look carefully enough, you will discover that the thoughts precede the thinker. So who is doing the actual thinking? No one. Thoughts happen. Consciousness thinks the way an apple tree apples. Thought is natural to consciousness; it is what consciousness does. There is no need for a thinker separate from consciousness to think the thoughts. There is just consciousness and thought.

That is why our wise sage made no attempt to get the prince to stop thinking he was a turkey. The boy could not control his thoughts, but he could control his behavior. The prince thought he was a turkey. Fine. Be a turkey. Just know that turkeys—at least wealthy, well-educated turkeys—function a lot like wealthy, well-educated princes.

Maybe you think you are turkey, or a loser, or a fool, or a crook. Fine. Leave the thoughts alone. Don't control your thoughts; control your behavior. Act holy, and in time you may discover thoughts supportive of these new behaviors. But even if you don't, at least you, too, will be a prince.

☐ The Turkey Prince

Reb Nachman of Breslov told this story:

A prince once took ill and thought he was a turkey. He refused to wear clothes and lived under the dining table, eating crumbs that fell to the floor. The king called upon the finest physicians, but none could find a cure. A wandering sage heard of the case and offered his services. The king agreed, and the sage removed his clothes and lived with the prince under the table, introducing himself to the prince as a fellow turkey.

After several weeks, the sage asked to wear a robe.

"What are you doing?" asked the Turkey Prince. "Turkeys don't wear robes."

"There is no law saying we turkeys cannot wear robes," the sage said, handing a robe to his friend. The prince thought for a moment, and then he, too, put on a robe.

A few days later the sage, dressed in his robe, had a complete meal served under the table.

"What are you doing now?" the Turkey Prince asked.

"There is no reason why we turkeys must live on scraps and crumbs when an entire meal is waiting for us." The prince joined the sage in his feast.

A week later when dinner was served, the sage chose to eat at the table sitting in a chair. Anticipating the query of the prince, the sage said, "There is no law prohibiting us turkeys from sitting at the table. Besides, it is much more comfortable to eat this way. Come and see for yourself." The prince did, and in time he recovered fully from his illness.

1 Baal Shem Tov (1698–1760): Rabbi Israel ben Eliezer was the founder of Hasidism. He began his public teaching in 1734 and soon earned the title Baal Shem Tov, Master of the Good Name (of God). He was an authentic healer of hearts, minds, and souls.

2 Shul: Synagogue.

3 Yom Kippur: Day of Atonement, when Jews confess and seek forgiveness before God.

4 Until age thirteen, one's sins fall upon one's parents. After age thirteen, one is responsible for oneself.

5 *Davvened:* Prayed.

6 Shepherds used whistles to call their sheep.

7 *Neilah:* The closing service of Yom Kippur. It is thought that at this time the Gates of Heaven are closing and we have one last chance to confess and ask for forgiveness. The service is marked by intense emotion.

ⓔ What is true prayer? Is it the recitation of sanctioned words and hymns? Is it the emotional outpouring of the heart? Is it the surrender of self to Self? It can be any of these, or none. The deciding factor is not so much what you do but the state of your heart as you do it. If you are half-hearted in your prayer, there is no praying. If you are whole-hearted in your prayer, there is praying even if that praying is nothing more than the loud blowing of a whistle.

☐ The Whistler

A tale is told of the Baal Shem Tov[1] and an illiterate villager's son. For the first thirteen years of the boy's life, his father never once took him to shul,[2] but on Yom Kippur[3] of his thirteenth year he did so for fear that otherwise his son would eat on this holy fast day and thus bring sin upon himself.[4]

All around him the men of the Baal Shem Tov's synagogue *davvened*[5] with great fervor, but not knowing anything about what they were doing, the boy grew bored. Feeling his herder's whistle[6] in his pocket, he asked his father if he could blow on it. Naturally, his father refused. Another hour passed, and again the boy asked for permission to play his whistle. Again his father refused, and he took the whistle from his son and placed it in his own pocket. As the *Neilah* service[7] began, the boy noticed the whistle sticking out of his father's pocket. He grabbed his whistle, took in a great gulp of air, and blew a long and loud blast.

Shocked and frightened by the sudden sound, the congregation fell silent. Only the Baal Shem Tov continued to *davven*, this time more joyously than before.

When the service concluded, the man took his son to apologize to the Baal Shem Tov for disrupting the service.

"On the contrary," the Baal Shem Tov said, "there was no disruption. The simplicity of the boy's blowing made my praying all the more easy for me."

@ We love systems: the Ten Commandments, the 613 *Mitzvos*, the Four Noble Truths, the Eightfold Path, the Twelve Steps. Systems give us a sense of security. If I just do "x," I am assured of attaining "y." Systems give us a sense of control: there is something to master, and mastery appeals to us. But here is Reb Zusya, who has yet to learn the Ten Principles of Divine Service, and his master, the *Maggid* of Mezritch, who does not even know how to teach them. Like all great spiritual truths, these ten principles cannot be taught but only observed and lived.

☐ The Child and the Thief

Reb Zusya of Hanipoli went to visit his rebbe, Reb Dov Ber, the *Maggid* of Mezritch.

"I have heard, Rebbe," Reb Zusya said, "that there are Ten Principles of Divine Service, but I have yet to learn what they are. I am hopeful that you can teach them to me."

Reb Dov Ber said, "I cannot teach them to you, but I can point to those who can."

"And who might these be?" asked Reb Zusya.

"You can learn the first three principles from a child and the next seven from a thief."

Seeing that Reb Zusya did not understand, the *Maggid* continued:

"From a child you can learn three things: be merry for no reason, never waste a moment's time, and demand what you want in a loud voice.

"And from a thief you can learn seven things: do your work in secret; if you do not complete a task one night, return to it the next; love your co-workers; risk your life to achieve your goal; be ready to exchange all you have for even the smallest gain; be willing to endure physical hardship; and be devoted to your work and give no thought to doing anything else."

1 *Dudelleh:* Yiddish for "you, my dear one."

@ This is the song of an awakened master. God is everywhere and everything. God embraces all duality in a greater nonduality. Good and bad, right and wrong, up and down, male and female, matter and spirit are all contained in the One Without Second. And if this is so, there is no way for us to define God at all.

God cannot be an idea. We can point toward an understanding of God through myth and metaphor, but God Him/Her/Itself is beyond any conceptualization. If we can think It, It cannot be God, for that would make God smaller than us.

God cannot be objectified. But God can be encountered. This is what Reb Levi Yitzchak experiences in this song. He never uses the word "God" or any of the Hebrew names for the Divine. He uses the familiar Yiddish *dudelleh*, "You, my dear one." The Yiddish carries with it a loving intimacy. Reb Levi Yitzchak isn't seeing God; he is embracing God. He isn't simply acknowledging God; he is loving God the way a child loves his mother when she plays peek-a-boo with him.

And this is what God is doing with you. Every moment, God, as it were, places God's hands over God's eyes and then removes them, pretending to see you as if for the first time and to be surprised. But it is you who is surprised: surprised to be seen, delighted to be seen, saved from an imagined loneliness, and embraced in an infinite love of seeing and being seen. When you can look and see, look and be seen, and know that the looker and the seer are both God, then you are awake to the game and ready to play another round.

☐ You!

Reb Levi Yitzchak of Berditchev used to sing this song, called *Dudelleh*:[1]

Where I wander—You!
Where I wonder—You!
Only You, You again, You always!
You! You! You!
When I am happy—You!
When I am sad—You!
Only You, You again, You always!
You! You! You!
Sky—You!
Earth—You!
You above!
You below!
In the beginning—You!
In the end—You!
Only You, You again, You always!
You! You! You!

@ Everyone hungers for a system that will take her to Truth. Everyone wants to know the formula that will bring him God-realization. Even if one chooses not to follow the path, it is supremely comforting to know that there is one. And that is what we all want: comfort. We want a God that is attainable. We want a God that is knowable. Ultimately, we want a God that is safe and controllable. But the true God is none of these things.

Torah tells us that God is *ehyeh asher ehyeh*, "I will be whatever I will be" (Exodus 3:14). God is infinite becoming, arising from infinite being. There is no way to God because God isn't anywhere but right here. There is no method for achieving God because God is already "yours." This is what the Zen people call "looking for an ox while riding on the ox." You already have the thing for which you are looking. What is needed is not *d'veikus*, union with God, but *da'at d'veikus*, realization of the union that already exists and always has.

What is your way to this realization? It must be your way, not another's. To follow another's way is to imitate truth, and a truth that is imitated is no longer true. The Seer of Lublin says that there are as many ways as there are people. If you are a student—study! If you are a devotee—pray! If you are an ascetic—fast! If you are an epicurean—feast!

The value of religion is that it preserves examples of the many ways to *da'at d'veikus*. The problem with religion is that it often insists that only one of these ways is legitimate. When it comes to spirituality, do not fall for "one size fits all." Find your size, and wear it proudly.

☐ Your Way

Reb Yissachar Dov of Radoshitz traveled to see his rebbe, Reb Yaakov Yitzchak, the *Chozeh* of Lublin. Arriving at his rebbe's study, he said, "Show me one general way that all of us might serve God."

"One way?" the Seer said. "What makes you think there is one way? Are people all the same that a single practice would suit them all?"

"Then how am I to teach people to find God?" Rebbe Yissachar Dov asked.

"It is impossible to tell people how they should serve. For one, the way is the way of study; for another, the way is the way of prayer; for another, the way is the way of fasting or feasting; for another, the way is the way of service to one's neighbor."

"Then what shall I tell those who ask me for guidance in this area?"

"Tell them this," the *Chozeh* said. "Carefully observe the way of your own heart, see what stirs your passion for God and godliness, and then do that with all your heart and all your strength."

Life is our rebbe. Ordinary things are our teachers. Reb Avraham Yaakov offers three examples. The train reminds us that each moment is precious and unique. If you are asleep to what is happening now, you cannot reclaim it later. The telegraph reminds us that words matter. A single word uttered in anger or spite can sour years of love and trust. Weigh the value of your words before speaking them. The telephone reminds us that distance is no defense against foolishness. "Here" and "there" are two ends of a single stick; do not think you can wave it here and not do damage there.

But there are other rebbes lurking in the ordinary things of everyday life:

A microwave: that which can heat up a meal can blow up a cat.

A television: that the foolishness of some can capture the imaginations of many.

Advertising: that the full can be made hungry simply with images.

Internet: that wisdom can be lost in too much information.

Religion: that disease must be learned before cures can be sold.

Politics: that serving leaders is much easier than servant leadership.

Look around you. Who are your rebbes? What are they teaching? What are you learning?

☐ Learn from Everything

Reb Avraham Yaakov of Sadigora was once sitting with his Hasidim. Their conversation was light and covered many topics. Almost as an aside, Reb Avraham Yaakov said, "You know, my friends, it is possible to learn great truths from even inanimate things. Everything can teach us something."

Taking the rebbe's statement as a challenge, one Hasid asked, "Tell me, Rebbe, what might we learn from a train?"

"That because of a single second you might miss the whole thing."

"And from a telegraph?" another student asked. "What might we learn from a telegraph?"

"That every word is counted, and that every word carries a cost."

"And the telephone, Rebbe," yet another Hasid asked. "Tell us what we can learn from this."

"That what you say here," Reb Avraham Yaakov said, "can surely be heard there."

1 *Kavvanot* (singular, *kavvanah*): The intellectual intentions one should focus on during various prayers and rituals.

2 *Ari:* An acronym for Holy Rabbi Yitzchak (Luria).

3 *Oy:* Yiddish exclamatory phrase.

@ Why is simplicity so rare? Because the ego thrives on complication.

Spirituality is simply the act of seeing what is. But to see clearly, we have to act simply. And this is the problem. We are taught that seeing is a complex act requiring a lifetime of study and rigorous practice. This is like someone shaking a jar of muddy water in the hope of catching a glimpse of a treasure hidden within it. What we need to do is put the jar down and allow the mud to settle to the bottom of its own accord. Then the water will clear, and you can see what the mud has hidden. But this seems too easy. After all, if things are that easy, why do we have such convoluted teachings and massive hierarchies of teachers? Could these serve only to keep the jar shaking, thus keeping the treasure hidden?

Life is complex but not complicated. The complexity of life reflects its diversity and creativity. The complications of life reflect our inability to be present and honest, kind and just.

☐ True Prayer

The Beadle of Rimanov, Rabbi Zvi Hirsch, came to his rebbe, Reb Menachem Mendel of Rimanov, to seek advice about a problem he was having during prayer.

"When I settle into my prayers," Reb Zvi Hirsch said, "I am distracted by flaming Hebrew letters and words. Whole sentences seem to flash before my eyes. It is impossible for me to concentrate on the prayer I am supposed to be praying."

"What you are seeing," Reb Menachem Mendel said, "are the innermost kavvanot[1] of our holy teacher, Rabbi Yitzchak Luria. You are receiving the deepest secrets hidden in the letters and words of the prayers you are praying. Others would give almost anything for such a gift, and you are complaining?"

"But Rebbe," Reb Zvi Hirsch said, "this is all well and good, and I have nothing but love and admiration for the Ari,[2] but all I want to do is concentrate on the simple meaning of the prayer."

Reb Menachem Mendel closed his eyes and sat quietly for a moment. "What you desire," he said in a half whisper, "is a very rare thing. One person in a generation can achieve what you are asking. To master the great secrets of prayer, to be privy to the kavvanot, and then to put it all aside to pray as a little child—oy![3]—if only this could be done, then would we know the Truth!"

[e] The word "remember" appears at least 125 times in the Hebrew Bible. This is what the Jewish philosopher and biblical scholar and translator Martin Buber calls a key word: a word whose frequent repetition is deliberate and intended to point us toward some important truth.

What does it mean to remember? You might think that the emphasis on remembering implies an almost obsessive concern with the past. Torah is calling us to live in the past, to conform to the past, to uphold the old as superior to the new. But where does remembering happen? Can you remember the past in the past? Of course not; all remembering takes place in the present. You cannot live in the past. You can live only in the present. You can, however, use the past as a veneer, an overlay that makes the present look like the past. You can repeat old patterns of thought and action to give yourself a sense of continuity with the past. Indeed, this is part and parcel of normative religion: to conform to the past in the present.

But this is not the only use of "remember." Reb Naftali was not seeking to remember the past but to be reminded of the present. He desired someone to call him back to this very moment and ask: For whom are you working? For yourself or for God?

The contemporary mystic and activist Andrew Harvey suggests you carry a small icon in your pocket to remember to return to the holy work of this moment. Torah suggests that you wear fringes on the corners of your garments to remind yourself of God and godliness (Numbers 15:38). The Vietnamese Zen master Thich Nhat Hanh suggests that you use the ringing of a bell or telephone as a call to return to the present. Reb Naftali hired a watchman. What will you do?

☐ The Reminderer

In the richer sections of Ropshitz, the town in which Reb Naftali was the rebbe, it was common for householders to hire night watchmen to guard their property. One evening, the rebbe went for a walk in the woods and returned to town through the neighborhood of the well-to-do. A watchman saw him coming through the forest and called for him to halt.

"I am sorry, Rebbe, I did not recognize you in the dark," the guard said as the rebbe drew closer to him under a gaslight.

The rebbe smiled and asked him, "For whom do you work?"

The watchman told him. Then he asked the rebbe the same question: "And for whom are you working this evening, Rebbe?"

The question hit Reb Naftali like a fist in his stomach. He stepped back a pace or two and then stammered, "I am not working for anyone at the moment."

The rebbe then began to pace back and forth under the gaslight. Suddenly he stopped, turned to the watchman, and said, "I would like to hire you."

"Me?" the man said. "I am a watchman. I know nothing of rebbes and their matters. I protect what matters to my master. What could I possibly do for you?"

"The very same," Reb Naftali said. "What matters to me is my soul, and to protect it I must work for God."

"But what would my job be?"

"To remind me," the rebbe said.

1 Elul: The month preceding Rosh Hashanah, the Jewish New Year. Normally coinciding with August–September, Elul is called the month of repentance, mercy, and forgiveness. The shofar is blown each morning of Elul with the exception of Shabbat morning, and Psalm 27 is read each day of the month. Elul is devoted to seeking forgiveness from people we may have hurt during the previous twelve months.

2 *Teshuvah* (Hebrew, "return"): The act of repentance. There are three steps to *teshuvah*. First, you must do what you can to make amends to the injured party. Second, you must feel contrition in your heart. Third, you must never repeat the hurtful action.

3 *Tikkun* (Hebrew, "repair"): There are two kinds of *tikkun*: *tikkun hanefesh,* repairing your soul, and *tikkun haolam,* repairing the world. The first consists of acts of *teshuvah,* getting yourself right with other people and with God. The second consists of social action, helping to set the world on a path toward justice and compassion.

@ Reb Chaim told this story during the month of Elul. His timing is significant. Elul is the month of forgiveness. It is during Elul that you speak with people, saying, "If I have hurt you in any way, knowingly or unknowingly, advertently or inadvertently, I ask for your forgiveness."

Asking for forgiveness reminds us that we are all lost in the forest of thoughtlessness and suffering. Reb Chaim is teaching us that we cannot escape from this forest alone. Only when we realize that we are all trapped in the selfishness of ego can we forgive one another and begin the trek home.

☐ Finding the Way

The Jewish month of Elul[1] is a time for deep *teshuvah*[2] and *tikkun*.[3] Reb Chaim Halberstam of Zanz once helped his Hasidim prepare for this journey by sharing this story:

"Once a woman became lost in a dense forest. She wandered this way and that in the hope of stumbling on a way out, but she only got more lost as the hours went by. Then she chanced upon another person walking in the woods. Hoping that he might know the way out, she said, 'Can you tell which path leads out of this forest?'

"'I am sorry, but I cannot,' the man said. 'I am quite lost myself.'

"'You have wandered in one part of the woods,' the woman said, 'while I have been lost in another. Together we may not know the way out, but we know quite a few paths that lead nowhere. Let us share what we know of the paths that fail, and then together we may find the one that succeeds.'

"What is true for these lost wanderers," Reb Chaim said, "is true of us as well. We may not know the way out, but let us share with each other the ways that have only led us back in."

[e] At the heart of Hasidic teaching is the realization that God is the source and substance of all reality. God is *Ayn Sof*, the Unbounded One. There is nothing that is not God, for if there were, then God would be limited and therefore no longer God.

This is a difficult idea for many people to grasp. We are so used to thinking in dualistic terms (subject and object, self and other) that we naturally think of God as the Absolute Other. But if this were so, we would be equal to God, being God's Absolute Other. If we are to understand what Yitzchak Meir knew even as a child, we need a new metaphor for God. Let me suggest the following:

A common tool in psychology is the concept of figure and ground, often represented by a graphic that can appear either as a goblet or as the profiles of two young women facing each other. Which image you see depends on where you place your attention. The seen image is called figure; the unseen is called ground. It is common to imagine that God is ground and creation is figure. But this is not what Yitzchak Meir knew. Both figure and ground are manifestations of yet a third unnamed and unknowable reality: the image itself when no one is looking at it. What is the IT that contains both the goblet and the young women? It is not other than them, nor is it reducible to them either singly or together. IT is that which cannot be seen, but which is absolutely necessary if anything is to see or be seen. IT is God, the unnamable reality. God is figure and ground and That Which Embraces Them Both.

☐ A Bet

When Rabbi Yitzchak Meir was a small child, his mother once took him to meet Reb Yisrael, the *Maggid* of Kosnitz. As they stood in line with the *Maggid*'s Hasidim, each waiting to see the holy rebbe, one of the disciples called to the young Yitzchak Meir.

"You mother tells us that you are quite bright and worthy of meeting our holy *Maggid*. But I am not so sure. So I will make a bet with you. I will give you a gulden if you can tell me where God lives!"

The Hasidim laughed at their fellow's jest. When their laughter faded, Yitzchak Meir looked up at the man and said, "And I will give you two gulden if you can tell me where God does not live!"

The Hasidim laughed even louder, and Yitzchak Meir and his mother were moved to the front of the line.

@ "Where am I?" This is the existential question Judaism places at the heart of human experience. Not "Who am I?" but "Where am I?" The difference between these two questions is critical.

"Who am I" sets the self in isolation. To answer this question, you must turn inward. Turning inward, you separate yourself from the world around you. "Where am I?" sets the self in relationship. To answer this question, you must turn both inward and outward; you must situate yourself in the world—both the world of self and the world of others. Indeed, to answer the question "Where" you must drop the notion of inward and outward altogether and see reality as a seamless whole of doing, feeling, thinking, and being.

When God calls to Adam in the Garden of Eden, Adam steps out of hiding and says, "I heard the sound of You in the Garden, and I was afraid, because I was naked; and I hid myself" (Genesis 3:10). Adam admits to both his feelings and his actions. He is aware of where he is both physically and emotionally. And with all his fears intact, he steps out of hiding.

This is the ultimate spiritual challenge. Without changing a thing, can you step out of hiding? Most of us imagine that we must change before we can be present to God. We need years of therapy, meditation, and spiritual discipline before we have earned the right to be present. But the truth is that there is nowhere else we can be. Right now, with all your fears, shame, mistakes, and muddleheadedness— just come out of hiding!

☐ Where Am I?

Reb Chanoch Henich of Alexander told this story:

"There was once a fellow who was very forgetful. Indeed, his memory was so short that when he awoke each morning he could not remember where he had laid his clothes the night before. Things got so bad for him that he could not fall asleep, so great was his nervousness about finding his things upon waking.

"One evening, however, he hit on a great idea. Taking pencil and paper, he wrote down exactly where he had placed each item of clothing. Placing his notes on the nightstand, by his bed, he quickly fell asleep, confident that he would find everything just perfectly in the morning.

"And indeed he did. He woke up, took the notes from his nightstand, and read off each item in turn: 'Pants—on chair back'; and there they were. He put them on. 'Shirt—on bed post'; and there it was. He put it on. 'Hat—on desk'; and there it sat. He placed it on his head. In a few minutes the fellow was completely dressed. But suddenly a great dread came upon him.

"'Yes, yes,' he said aloud. 'Here are my pants, my shirt, and my cap; but where am I?'

"He looked and looked and looked, but he could find himself nowhere."

Reb Chanoch Henich paused for a moment and then concluded, "And that is how it is with each of us as well."

☐ Suggested Readings

Buber, Martin. *Hasidism and Modern Man.* New York: Harper Torchbooks, 1966.

———. *The Origin and Meaning of Hasidism.* New York: Harper Torchbooks, 1966.

———. *Tales of the Hasidim.* New York: Schocken Books, 1975.

———. *The Way of Man: According to the Teaching of Hasidism.* Secaucus, N.J.: Carol Publishing, 1998.

Buxbaum, Yitzhak. *Jewish Tales of Holy Women.* San Francisco: Jossey-Bass, 2002.

———. *Jewish Tales of Mystic Joy.* San Francisco: Jossey-Bass, 2002.

Citron, Sterna. *Why the Baal Shem Tov Laughed: Fifty-two Stories about Our Great Chasidic Rabbis.* Northdale, N.J.: Jason Aronson, 1993.

Finkel, Avraham Yaakov. *Great Chasidic Masters.* Northdale, N.J.: Jason Aronson, 1992.

Frankel, Ellen. *The Classic Tales: Four Thousand Years of Jewish Lore.* Northdale, N.J.: Jason Aronson, 1989.

Kaplan, Aryeh. *Chasidic Masters: History, Biography, Thought.* New York: Maznaim Publishing, 1984.

Levin, Meyer. *Classic Hassidic Tales: Marvellous Tales of Rabbi Israel Baal Shem and of His Great-Grandson, Rabbi Nachman, Retold from Hebrew, Yiddish, and German.* New York: Penguin Books, 1975.

Newman, Louis. *The Hasidic Anthology: Tales and Teachings of the Hasidim.* Northdale, N.J.: Jason Aronson, 1987.

Patai, Joseph. *Souls and Secrets: Hasidic Stories.* Translated by Raphael Patai. Northdale, N.J.: Jason Aronson, 1995.

Polsky, Howard, and Yaella Wozner. *Everyday Miracles: The Healing Wisdom of Hasidic Stories.* Northdale, N.J.: Jason Aronson, 1989.

Raphael, Yitzhak. *Sefer HaChasidut* (Hebrew). Tel Aviv: A. Zioni Publishing, 1961.

Schochet, Jacob Immanuel. *Tzava'at Harivash.* New York: Kehot Publication Society, 1998.

Schram, Penninah, ed. *Chosen Tales: Stories Told by Jewish Storytellers.* Northvale, N.J.: Jason Aronson, 1997.

Wiesel, Elie. *Somewhere a Master.* New York: Summit Books, 1982.

———. *Souls on Fire.* Northdale, N.J.: Jason Aronson, 1993.

Zevin, S.Y. *Sippurei Chasadim* (Hebrew). Jerusalem, 2000.

———. *A Treasury of Chassidic Tales on the Festivals.* Translated by Uri Kaploun. New York: Mesorah Publications, 1983.

———. *A Treasury of Chassidic Tales on the Torah.* Translated by Uri Kaploun. New York: Mesorah Publications, 1983.

About SKYLIGHT PATHS Publishing

SkyLight Paths Publishing is creating a place where people of different spiritual traditions come together for challenge and inspiration, a place where we can help each other understand the mystery that lies at the heart of our existence.

Through spirituality, our religious beliefs are increasingly becoming a part of our lives—rather than *apart* from our lives. While many of us may be more interested than ever in spiritual growth, we may be less firmly planted in traditional religion. Yet, we do want to deepen our relationship to the sacred, to learn from our own as well as from other faith traditions, and to practice in new ways.

SkyLight Paths sees both believers and seekers as a community that increasingly transcends traditional boundaries of religion and denomination—people wanting to learn from each other, *walking together, finding the way.*

We at SkyLight Paths take great care to produce beautiful books that present meaningful spiritual content in a form that reflects the art of making high quality books. Therefore, we want to acknowledge those who contributed to the production of this book.

PRODUCTION
Tim Holtz & Bridgett Taylor

EDITORIAL
Maura D. Shaw & Emily Wichland

COVER DESIGN
Walter C. Bumford III, Stockton, Massachusetts

TEXT DESIGN
Chelsea Cloeter, River Forest, Illinois

PRINTING & BINDING
Versa Press, East Peoria, Illinois

 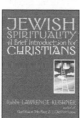  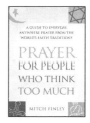

Spiritual Practice

Women Pray
Voices through the Ages, from Many Faiths, Cultures, and Traditions
Edited and with introductions by *Monica Furlong*

Many ways—new and old—to communicate with the Divine.

This beautiful gift book celebrates the rich variety of ways women around the world have called out to the Divine—with words of joy, praise, gratitude, wonder, petition, longing, and even anger—from the ancient world up to our own time. Prayers from women of nearly every religious or spiritual background give us an eloquent expression of what it means to communicate with God. 5 x7¼, 256 pp, Deluxe HC with ribbon marker, ISBN 1-893361-25-X **$19.95**

Praying with Our Hands: *Twenty-One Practices of Embodied Prayer from the World's Spiritual Traditions*
by *Jon M. Sweeney;* Photographs by *Jennifer J. Wilson;*
Foreword by *Mother Tessa Bielecki;* Afterword by *Taitetsu Unno, Ph.D.*

A spiritual guidebook for bringing prayer into our bodies.

This inspiring book of reflections and accompanying photographs shows us twenty-one simple ways of using our hands to speak to God, to enrich our devotion and ritual. All express the various approaches of the world's religious traditions to bringing the body into worship. Spiritual traditions represented include Anglican, Sufi, Zen, Roman Catholic, Yoga, Shaker, Hindu, Jewish, Pentecostal, Eastern Orthodox, and many others.
8 x 8, 96 pp, 22 duotone photographs, Quality PB, ISBN 1-893361-16-0 **$16.95**

  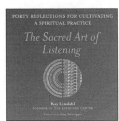 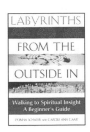

The Sacred Art of Listening
Forty Reflections for Cultivating a Spiritual Practice
by *Kay Lindahl;* Illustrations by *Amy Schnapper*

More than ever before, we need to embrace the skills and practice of listening. You will learn to: Speak clearly from your heart • Communicate with courage and compassion • Heighten your awareness for deep listening • Enhance your ability to listen to people with different belief systems. 8 x 8, 160 pp, Illus., Quality PB, ISBN 1-893361-44-6 **$16.95**

Labyrinths from the Outside In
Walking to Spiritual Insight—a Beginner's Guide
by *Donna Schaper* and *Carole Ann Camp*

The user-friendly, interfaith guide to making and using labyrinths— for meditation, prayer, and celebration.

Labyrinth walking is a spiritual exercise *anyone* can do. This accessible guide unlocks the mysteries of the labyrinth for all of us, providing ideas for using the labyrinth walk for prayer, meditation, and celebrations to mark the most important moments in life. Includes instructions for making a labyrinth of your own and finding one in your area.
6 x 9, 208 pp, b/w illus. and photographs, Quality PB, ISBN 1-893361-18-7 **$16.95**

Kabbalah

Honey from the Rock
An Introduction to Jewish Mysticism
by *Lawrence Kushner*

An insightful and absorbing introduction to the ten gates of Jewish mysticism and how it applies to daily life. "The easiest introduction to Jewish mysticism you can read."
6 x 9, 176 pp, Quality PB, ISBN 1-58023-073-3 **$16.95**

Eyes Remade for Wonder
The Way of Jewish Mysticism and Sacred Living
A Lawrence Kushner Reader
Intro. by *Thomas Moore*, author of *Care of the Soul*

Whether you are new to Kushner or a devoted fan, you'll find inspiration here. With samplings from each of Kushner's works, and a generous amount of new material, this book is to be read and reread, each time discovering deeper layers of meaning in our lives.
6 x 9, 240 pp, Quality PB, ISBN 1-58023-042-3 **$18.95**; HC, ISBN 1-58023-014-8 **$23.95**

Invisible Lines of Connection
Sacred Stories of the Ordinary
by *Lawrence Kushner* AWARD WINNER!

Through his everyday encounters with family, friends, colleagues and strangers, Kushner takes us deeply into our lives, finding flashes of spiritual insight in the process.
5¼ x 8¼, 160 pp, Quality PB, ISBN 1-879045-98-3 **$15.95**

  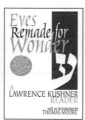  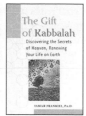

Finding Joy
A Practical Spiritual Guide to Happiness
by *Dannel I. Schwartz* with *Mark Hass* AWARD WINNER!

Explains how to find joy through a time honored, creative—and surprisingly practical— approach based on the teachings of Jewish mysticism and Kabbalah.
6 x 9, 192 pp, Quality PB, ISBN 1-58023-009-1 **$14.95**; HC, ISBN 1-879045-53-2 **$19.95**

The Gift of Kabbalah:
Discovering the Secrets of Heaven, Renewing Your Life on Earth
by *Tamar Frankiel*, Ph.D.

Makes accessible the mysteries of Kabbalah. Traces Kabbalah's evolution in Judaism and shows us its most important gift: a way of revealing the connection between our "everyday" life and the spiritual oneness of the universe.
6 x 9, 256 pp, Quality PB, ISBN 1-58023-141-1 **$16.95**; HC, ISBN 1-58023-108-X **$21.95**

Children's Spirituality

MULTICULTURAL, NONDENOMINATIONAL, NONSECTARIAN

Ten Amazing People
And How They Changed the World

For ages 7–10

by *Maura D. Shaw*; Foreword by *Dr. Robert Coles*
Full-color illus. by *Stephen Marchesi*

Black Elk • Dorothy Day • Malcolm X • Mahatma Gandhi • Martin Luther King, Jr. • Mother Teresa • Janusz Korczak • Desmond Tutu • Thich Nhat Hanh • Albert Schweitzer

This vivid, inspirational, and authoritative book will open new possibilities for children by telling the stories of how ten of the past century's greatest leaders changed the world in important ways.
8½, x 11, 48 pp, HC, Full-color illus., ISBN 1-893361-47-0 **$17.95**

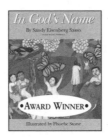

God's Paintbrush

For ages 4 & up

by *Sandy Eisenberg Sasso*; Full-color illus. by *Annette Compton*
Invites children of all faiths and backgrounds to encounter God openly in their own lives. Wonderfully interactive; provides questions adult and child can explore together at the end of each episode. "An excellent way to honor the imaginative breadth and depth of the spiritual life of the young." —Dr. Robert Coles, Harvard University
11 x 8½, 32 pp, HC, Full-color illus., ISBN 1-879045-22-2 **$16.95**

Also available:
A Teacher's Guide 8½ x 11, 32 pp, PB, ISBN 1-879045-57-5 **$8.95**
God's Paintbrush Celebration Kit 9½ x 12, HC, Includes 5 sessions/40 full-color Activity Sheets and Teacher Folder with complete instructions, ISBN 1-58023-050-4 **$21.95**

In God's Name

For ages 4 & up

by *Sandy Eisenberg Sasso*; Full-color illus. by *Phoebe Stone*
Like an ancient myth in its poetic text and vibrant illustrations, this award-winning modern fable about the search for God's name celebrates the diversity and, at the same time, the unity of all the people of the world. "What a lovely, healing book!" —Madeleine L'Engle
9 x 12, 32 pp, HC, Full-color illus., ISBN 1-879045-26-5 **$16.95**

Also available in Spanish:
El nombre de Dios 9 x 12, 32 pp, HC, Full-color illus., ISBN 1-893361-63-2 **$16.95**

Where Does God Live?

For ages 3–6

by *August Gold* and *Matthew J. Perlman*
Using simple, everyday examples that children can relate to, this colorful book helps young readers develop a personal understanding of God.
10 x 8½, 32 pp, Quality PB, Full-color photo illus., ISBN 1-893361-39-X **$8.95**

Spiritual Perspectives

Explores how spiritual beliefs can inform our opinions and transform our actions in areas of social justice and societal change. Tackling the most important—and most divisive—issues of our day, this series provides easy-to-understand introductions to contemporary issues. Readers aren't told what to think; rather, they're given information—*spiritual* perspectives—in order to reach their own conclusions.

Spiritual Perspectives on America's Role as Superpower
by *the Editors at SkyLight Paths*

Are we the world's good neighbor or a global bully?

Explores broader issues surrounding the use of American power around the world, including in Iraq and the Middle East. From a spiritual perspective, what are America's responsibilities as the only remaining superpower? Contributors:

Dr. Beatrice Bruteau • Rev. Dr. Joan Brown Campbell • Tony Campolo • Rev. Forrest Church • Lama Surya Das • Matthew Fox • Kabir Helminski • Thich Nhat Hanh • Eboo Patel • Abbot M. Basil Pennington, ocso • Dennis Prager • Rosemary Radford Ruether • Wayne Teasdale • Rev. William McD. Tully • Rabbi Arthur Waskow • John Wilson
5½ x 8½, 256 pp, Quality PB, ISBN 1-893361-81-0 **$16.95**

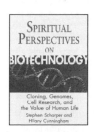
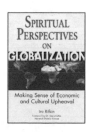

Spiritual Perspectives on Biotechnology
Cloning, Genomes, Cell Research, and the Value of Human Life
by *Stephen Scharper and Hilary Cunningham*

A balanced introduction to the issues of biotechnology.

From genetically modified foods through cloning of animals and life forms, explains in clear and nonjudgmental language the beliefs that motivate religious leaders, activists, theologians, academics, and others involved on all sides of biotechnology issues. Many different perspectives are included—representing all of the world's largest faith traditions and many other spiritual persuasions.
5½ x 8½, 235 pp, Quality PB, ISBN 1-893361-58-6 **$16.95**

Spiritual Perspectives on Globalization
Making Sense of Economic and Cultural Upheaval
by *Ira Rifkin*; Foreword by *Dr. David Little, Harvard Divinity School*

What is globalization? What are spiritually-minded people saying and doing about it?

This lucid introduction surveys the religious landscape, explaining in clear and nonjudgmental language the beliefs that motivate spiritual leaders, activists, theologians, academics, and others involved on all sides of the issue.
5½ x 8½, 224 pp, Quality PB, ISBN 1-893361-57-8 **$16.95**

Religious Etiquette/Reference

How to Be a Perfect Stranger, 3rd Edition
The Essential Religious Etiquette Handbook
Edited by *Stuart M. Matlins* and *Arthur J. Magida*

The indispensable guidebook to help the well-meaning guest when visiting other people's religious ceremonies.

A straightforward guide to the rituals and celebrations of the major religions and denominations in the United States and Canada from the perspective of an interested guest of any other faith, based on information obtained from authorities of each religion. Belongs in every living room, library, and office.

COVERS:

African American Methodist Churches • Assemblies of God • Baha'i • Baptist • Buddhist • Christian Church (Disciples of Christ) • Christian Science (Church of Christ, Scientist) • Churches of Christ • Episcopalian and Anglican • Hindu • Islam • Jehovah's Witnesses • Jewish • Lutheran • Mennonite/Amish • Methodist • Mormon (Church of Jesus Christ of Latter-day Saints) • Native American/First Nations • Orthodox Churches • Pentecostal Church of God • Presbyterian • Quaker (Religious Society of Friends) • Reformed Church in America/Canada • Roman Catholic • Seventh-day Adventist • Sikh • Unitarian Universalist • United Church of Canada • United Church of Christ 6 x 9, 432 pp, Quality PB, ISBN 1-893361-67-5 **$19.95**

Also available:

The Perfect Stranger's Guide to Funerals and Grieving Practices
A Guide to Etiquette in Other People's Religious Ceremonies
Edited by *Stuart M. Matlins*
6 x 9, 240 pp, Quality PB, ISBN 1-893361-20-9 **$16.95**

The Perfect Stranger's Guide to Wedding Ceremonies
A Guide to Etiquette in Other People's Religious Ceremonies
Edited by *Stuart M. Matlins*
6 x 9, 208 pp, Quality PB, ISBN 1-893361-19-5 **$16.95**

Or phone, fax, mail or e-mail to: SKYLIGHT PATHS Publishing
Sunset Farm Offices, Route 4 • P.O. Box 237 • Woodstock, Vermont 05091
Tel: (802) 457-4000 • Fax: (802) 457-4004 • www.skylightpaths.com
Credit card orders: (800) 962-4544 (8:30AM–5:30PM ET Monday–Friday)
Generous discounts on quantity orders. SATISFACTION GUARANTEED. Prices subject to change.